THE MEANING OF DREAMS

THE MEANING OF DREAMS

BY

ELLIOTT O'DONNELL

GYAN

ISBN : 978-81-212-1788-0 (HB)

First Published, 1899

Published, 2018

Published by

Gyan Publishing House
5, Ansari Road
Daryaganj, New Delhi-110002
Phone: 011-47034999, 9811692060
www.gyanbooks.com
E-mail: books@gyanbooks.com

GYAN

Printed at: G. Print Process, Delhi.

PREFACE

My interpretation of dreams in this volume is based on my own experiences and the experiences of certain people with whom I have come in contact.

ELLIOTT O'DONNELL

14 Becondale Road, Gipsy Hill, S.E.
July 29, 1911

CONTENTS

PART I

EVERY NIGHT DREAMS

CHAP.		PAGE
I.	Animal Dreams	9
II.	Accidents, Births, Balloons, &c.	46
III.	The Naked Dream, &c.	64

PART II

OUT OF THE ORDINARY DREAMS

IV.	Dreams of the Afflicted, &c.	81
V.	Phantastic Dreams	93
VI.	Repetitionary and Peculiarly Vivid Dreams	125
VII.	Tale Dreams	151
INDEX		193

PART I

EVERY NIGHT DREAMS

CHAPTER I

ANIMAL DREAMS

To dream of a flying bat means an impending catastrophe (not infrequently from water), but not necessarily to the dreamer. To dream of a motionless bat means some impending illness of a more or less serious nature, but not necessarily of the dreamer. If, however, the sleeper dreams the bat settles on him, then he himself will be the sufferer either from some physical injury or from some grievous sickness. To exemplify my theory that bats portend disaster in a greater or a less degree, I will quote a few cases I have collected for that purpose. A lady, whom I will designate Miss Spenser, once dreamed she was crossing a hayfield when she heard a loud buzzing overhead, and, on looking up, perceived a number of bats some feet above her, engaged in whirling round and round in a state of hopeless chaos and confusion. Presently they swooped down, swirled round and round her face, though never near enough to touch her, and whilst they were still swirling, she awoke. A day or two afterwards, her favourite sister was drowned in Lake Lucerne.

A Major Roper, writing to me some time ago from India, said : " Here is an experience that may be useful to you in compiling your work on dreams. I have twice dreamed of bats, and on each occasion the dream has been followed by a calamity. In the first instance, I thought I was sitting in my bedroom in my old home in Bedford (I am an old B.G.S. boy), when six bats, one after the other, flew in at the window, and, after whizzing round the room, vanished in the marvellous fashion that seems so natural in a dream. The next day I had a cablegram from England to say my brother was drowned while bathing in the sea.

" The other dream, which occurred only last year, was to this effect : I was riding outside an omnibus in London when a bat suddenly flew past me. All my fellow-passengers cried out in a chorus, ' How remarkable ! A bat ! ' and I awoke actually repeating those words. I was so impressed that I jotted down the dream in my memorandum book. Exactly a week later, I received tidings of my father's death : he had been thrown from a trap, whilst descending a steep hill near Dublin, and killed on the spot."

In reference to motionless bats; a lady informed me, that one night she dreamed her counterpane was covered with bats, and bats being her pet aversion; she was so terrified that she immediately awoke, to find her whole body bathed in perspiration. The following day, she learned that an aunt to whom she was greatly attached had been taken seriously ill, and within the week she received the news that her aunt was dead.

Another lady once dreamed she saw her youngest sister lying on the grass, apparently asleep, with two bats on her face. With a cry of dismay, for she loathed bats, my friend picked up a spade, the first thing that came to hand, to knock them off, when the scene changed, and she found herself digging a grave! She awoke in terror, and two days later heard of the death of her youngest sister, who had succumbed under an operation for appendicitis.

Writing to me from Gipsy Hill, Norwood, a lady said: "My sister Mabel once dreamed a bat settled on her shoulder, and she could not get it off. She awoke in a great fright, she told me, and she could not help feeling that the dream prognosticated something unpleasant. Her presentiment, unhappily, was only too correct, for shortly afterwards she caught a severe chill which terminated in a fatal attack of pneumonia.

BEARS

Bears have always been associated with the unpleasant side of the occult. Those, however, that made such short work of Elisha's tormentors; although undoubtedly psychic (since to appear and cause to disappear with such startling suddenness is only characteristic of the superphysical), were to my mind far more opportune than they were unpleasant. Indeed, I might go further and confess that I should not be extremely sorry were such a demonstration of the occult bear, as that recorded in the Scriptures, to take place periodically amongst the ill-mannered and superfluous children of to-day. Many places are said to be haunted by evil spirits in ursine guise. I have myself visited a house in Chelsea where the apparition of a shaggy bear is seen, and it is a well-known fact that the Tower of London was once (and perhaps still is) haunted by the phantasm of a bear. A young man once told me that he dreamed a huge shaggy bear, with an intensely diabolical expression in its little brown eyes, entered his room, and, approaching the foot of his bed, reared itself on its hind legs and peered at him. In a great state of alarm, he got out of bed, and had almost reached the window-sill, when the bear stalked up to him; and, placing its paws on his shoulders, deliberately breathed into his face. He awoke with its hot breath burning into his brain, and from that night, he assured me, he was a changed man; and, one bad act leading to another, he was at length smuggled out of the country to escape jail.

A destitute girl I once befriended on the Thames Embankment, and who, in return for the supper I gave her at a neighbouring restaurant, stole the teaspoons, told me she was quite certain she owed her downfall to the sinister influence of a dream.

"I was in a shop in Oxford Street at the time," she said, "and beyond being rather fond of flirtations and dress, as most girls are, I had never done any serious wrong. One night, however, I dreamed I was at a ball and my partner was a bear. He danced divinely and I fell in love with him. He very politely asked permission to see me home, and, on arriving outside the shop, suddenly kissed me; and, with the moisture of his nasty wet mouth still on my lips, I awoke. Well, try how I would I could not banish that dream from my mind. I saw the bear always, no matter whether I was at work or taking my recreation, my thoughts were always of him; and the result was—I became thoroughly demoralised. I quarrelled with the young man to whom I was engaged, and got engaged to someone else, and within six months terminated that engagement and 'took on' with a third. I had no pity for the men I jilted, but laughed in their faces when they upbraided me, and took a fiendish delight in parading about with my latest lover in the face of the one I had just discarded. I spent money recklessly, and when I got in debt—I stole! The end of it all was I was sent to prison, and when I came out I drifted—anywhere. And I am sure I owe it all, all my folly and subsequent blinding damning misery, to the dream of that bear—that cursed, fascinating, hellish bear."

I think these two illustrations will suffice to show the significance of bear-dreams in general.

BIRDS

Bird-dreams are very common. With them alone I might fill a volume. However, as my space is not unlimited, I can only deal briefly with a few of them.

To dream of canary birds signifies good fortune in the shape of money—either a legacy, a rise in salary, or a present. Whereas to dream about doves implies good fortune of any other than a pecuniary nature, such, for example, as recovery from illness, success in work or success in love affairs.

To dream of a cuckoo means an unexpected find, as, for instance, the picking up of coins or other valuables in the street, or the finding of something that has long been lost.

Crows in dreams are harbingers of bad luck, and import losses, pecuniary and otherwise, quarrels and disappointments.

Ducks, on the other hand, portend good fortune, presents, and kisses.

Fowls imply quarrels ; geese new dresses.

To dream about eagles implies great success ; whereas to dream of vultures portends failure and illness.

Magpies, whether single or in numbers, mean death—if in flight, the death of some acquaintance or relative ; if motionless, the death of the dreamer.

To dream of hawks signifies the making of an enemy ; to dream of owls implies the breaking of a friendship, the breaking off of an engagement, serious illness, accident, or death.

Parrots in dreams are significant of impending

scandal and gossip; pigeons are significant of presents of all kinds.

Ravens portend grave misfortunes, and not nfrequently the near presence of some phantasm; sparrows signify petty losses and quarrels; swallows portend grief—grief at someone's illness, misfortunes or death—but grief, invariably grief.

Storks in dreams mean an approaching birth; wrens an approaching engagement or marriage.

The following are a few of the many accounts of bird-dreams upon which I have based my assumptions:

A lady writing to me from Southsea says: "I am sure that canaries in dreams are significant of extreme good fortune. Two years ago, I dreamed a canary dashed against my window-pane, and the very next morning I received a handsome cheque from an uncle, with whom I had held no sort of communication for years. The night before last, I dreamed a couple of canaries flew round my bed singing, and, coming down to breakfast in the morning, I found a letter awaiting me from a solicitor to say that my godfather had died suddenly and had left me a substantial legacy."

A girl whose age I dare not state, lest some at least of my readers should deem her precocious, informs me that she likes to dream of ducks!

"They mean so much!" "I dreamed of ducks a week ago," she boldly confided to me, "and the following evening my cousin, George—he is not really my cousin, you know—he is a middy, and I secretly adore him—kissed me! I felt certain he was in love, only he was too shy to say anything and—well, I never thought he would have clinched matters so precipitately. But my duck-dreams are always good. When I dreamed of them once before; what do you think I got in the morning? Why, a gold watch from a great-aunt, who had never in her life before made me a present of anything. So, you see, I just mean to dream of ducks as often as I can."

The experience of an elderly married lady, who until recently resided in Upper Norwood, is not so pleasant. "I dread either seeing or dreaming of magpies," she said to me; "they always foretell a death. I dreamed three magpies crossed my path the day before my father died, and I dreamed one huge magpie flew in at the door and perched on one of the knobs at the foot of my bed, exactly a week before the death of my eldest son."

I, too, have dreamed of magpies, and, as in the case I have just quoted, the dreams have always occurred shortly before a death. The night a very near relative of mine died, I dreamed a large number of magpies flew in at my window; and the day before a dog to which I was very much attached was run over and killed, I dreamed two magpies settled on my shoulder, and that I could not make them go.

Also, when I was living in a big, rambling house in Cornwall, I dreamed a raven flew down the chimney and pecked me vigorously three times on the hand. Indeed, the pecks hurt me so much that I awoke. Everything was very quiet and the room pitch dark. I was turning over to try sleeping on my other side, when I suddenly saw a light, and, on looking up, perceived, to my surprise and terror, the luminous face of a diabolical old hag pressed against the window, which was at least thirty feet from the ground. Having slept in the house for several months without seeing anything abnormal, I had hitherto attributed the rumour that it was haunted to the superstition of the peasantry, in the first place, and, in the second place; to their insatiable love of foolish gossip.

Now, however, as I gazed at the hideous countenance, and rubbed my eyes to make sure I was not dreaming, I felt that the gossip I had scorned was only too well founded, and I determined that nothing should induce me to sleep in that room again. The apparition was only visible for a very few seconds, and when I stirred it completely vanished. I have not only experienced this percursor of the occult myself, but I know others who have dreamed of ravens shortly before witnessing an occult phenomenon.

I dreamed of a wren just before I got engaged to be married; and three of my correspondents always dream they see a wren prior to hearing of a marriage. Larks portend good news of friends and relations, and happy events generally. Linnets portend marriages; thrushes minor ailments and troubles.

BULLS

To dream of being chased by a bull portends some accident, such as breakage or loss, seldom anything more serious. For example, I see in one of my letters that a gentleman dreamed he was chased along the Marine Parade at Worthing by a bull, the day before one of his most valuable china ornaments was broken; and, referring to another letter, I see that a lady in Clifton dreamed a bull ran after her in Guthrie Road, and tossed her over the railings of Emmanuel Church, the day before one of her servants fell downstairs and broke the larger part of a valuable tea-set of Worcester china.

CATS

To dream of a white cat is lucky; of a black, either extremely lucky or the reverse; of a tabby, neither lucky nor unlucky; of a tortoiseshell, simply disastrous.

Of the many cat dreams that have from time to time been related to me, I think the following are the best examples:

Mrs. Smith, who resides in the neighbourhood of Haverstock Hill, Hampstead, writes to me thus:

"My daughters and I have on several occasions dreamed of white cats, and our dreams have always been the precursors of astonishing pieces of good luck. Daisy, my eldest daughter, dreamed a black cat sprang on her shoulder and refused to stir, the night before she received tidings that her picture was on the line in the Royal Academy. Vera, my second girl, dreamed she was punting on a lake, which was overcrowded with white cats, that swam about with the keenest enjoyment, every now and then boarding her craft and rubbing their noses caressingly against her; and, a day or two later, she received a quite unexpected invitation to accompany a friend on a yachting voyage to the Baltic. And now for my own experience. The night before my husband presented me with a magnificent sealskin coat, when I all but collapsed with astonishment, I dreamed that a big black cat was sitting on a chest of drawers in my room, and that directly it saw me, it leaped into the middle of the room and sank through the floor."

A striking example of the cat-dream that is invariably, with some people, followed by misfortune, occurred to a lady I met in Llandudno. "Shortly before my father lost most of his money in a big bank smash," she said, "I dreamed I saw a tortoiseshell cat on the mantelshelf. And again a day or two prior to my husband's loss of half his fortune in the failure of an American mine, I dreamed I was bitten by a tortoiseshell cat. Hence; I consider dreaming of a tortoiseshell cat a very bad augury."

Speaking from my own experience, I have found dreams of black cats unlucky. For instance, the night before I had an accident on the stage, I dreamed a huge black cat persistently followed me out of doors, and that when I tried to drive it away it scratched me. And again, before I received an injury in one of my eyes, I dreamed a black cat flew out of a wood and clawed a hole in my hand. And yet again, before I lost a train which it was of vital importance for me to catch, I dreamed a black cat upset an inkpot all over a suit I had just bought, completely ruining it."

COWS

Cows in dreams appear to be lucky omens in general, and especially portend unexpected visits from friends. One lady, I know, has always dreamed of cows, prior to receiving an unexpected visit from any old friend, whom she has not seen for years.

CROCODILES

To dream of crocodiles foretells danger from drowning, and lightning. Also sorrow at the loss of a friend.

DEER

Dreams about deer presage trouble with the eyes, missing trains, and petty annoyances.

DOGS

Dog-dreams, as may be supposed, are very general. There are probably few people who have not dreamed them. But as there are many kinds of dogs, and each species in dreamland conveys a separate meaning, I can only signal out a few for interpretation.

Briefly, then :

Boarhounds in dreams presage riding accidents or accidents at sea ; bloodhounds, serious reverses ; collies, the breaking of friendships through deceit and treachery ; dachshunds, unexpected rencontres with friends ; greyhounds; illnesses or deaths ; foxhounds, tidings from unexpected quarters ; mastiffs, danger from fire ; Pomeranians, danger from robbers, burglars, and street ruffians ; spaniels, the breaking off of engagements, and disappointments in general ; terriers, petty successes or quarrels.

Among the many dog dreams that have been narrated to me, the following are, perhaps, the most noteworthy. A lady I met some few years ago dreamed she was walking down Bond Street, when a greyhound suddenly leaped from off the roof of one of the houses and fell in a heap at her feet. She then saw to her horror that it was metamorphosed into her father, and, sure enough, the very next day, she received a telegram to say that her father had died, quite unexpectedly, in the night. She also dreamed, a day or two before the death of her greatest friend, that she was travelling by rail with two greyhounds seated opposite her in the same compartment. Another person told me; that, shortly before a fire in her house, she had a curious dream about a mastiff. The creature entered the room in which she was sitting, and suddenly flew at the hearthrug and tore it to pieces. Another lady I once questioned as to her dreams informed me that she had been engaged three times, and that prior to the termination of each engagement she had dreamed of a dachshund. There are grimmer stories in connection with Pomeranians. One man I met told me that he once dreamed he saw his little boy worried to death in the most horrible manner by a Pomeranian dog, and that, on the following evening, his house was broken into by burglars.

Another person—if I remember rightly, an Anglo-Indian doctor—once told me that he dreamed he was alone in a very gloomy church, and that a gigantic man in a black surplice suddenly appeared in the pulpit, and, after making the most hideous faces was transformed into a monstrous Pomeranian dog. What happened then the dreamer could not recollect, but he thinks it must have been something very alarming, as he was bathed in perspiration when he literally awoke to the fact that his bed was gently rising beneath him. Unable to determine whether he was still dreaming, he gave himself a sharp pinch and sat up, whereupon something crawled from under him and made a precipitate bolt for the door. Knowing now that he had to deal with something material, the doctor lost no time, but whipping up his revolver, which he always kept under his pillow, and aiming at random, he fired three or four times in rapid succession. Probably the last of these shots took effect, for it was immediately followed by a dull thud on the floor. On the arrival of the rest of the household, with lights, the intruder was seen to be a coolie who had formerly been in the doctor's employ but had been discharged for theft. He at once confessed that he had hidden there early in the evening, when the doctor was at dinner, with the intention of robbing and murdering his former employer, but, being overcome with exhaustion, he had fallen into a stupor, from which he was just rousing himself when the doctor felt the bed move. Having dreamed of a Pomeranian dog prior to the other occasion upon which the coolies had stolen articles from his bungalow, the doctor came to the conclusion that, as far as he was concerned at all events, dreams about dogs of that species signified robbery, if nothing worse.

DONKEYS

To dream of donkeys presages minor trouble and ailments.

FISH

Here again the subject of fish-dreams is a very large one, far too large for me to deal with very exhaustively. I must therefore, as in the case of the bird and dog dreams, be content with a few selections.

To dream about gold and silver fish is distinctly fortunate, and points to legacies and presents, chiefly monetary.

To dream about whales is indicative of impending law suits, debts, bankruptcy, and pecuniary difficulties.

To dream about sharks portends death, illness, or an enemy. To dream about mackerel imports coming domestic bothers; about herring, pleasures in the shape of visits to friends or places of entertainment; about sprats, children's ailments; about pike, quarrels; about flat fish (generally speaking), misfortunes in some form or another, but seldom deaths; about salmon; unexpected success; happiness, presents, and the forming of sound friendships; about minnows and sticklebacks, petty quarrels, and disappointments ; about eels; ruptures in love affairs; nasty " turns " by enemies; failures in work.

I have often dreamed about fish. I remember once having a very vivid dream about a shark. I fancied I was bathing in a fresh-water pool close to the house where I was staying, when, to my surprise and horror, I suddenly saw the fin of a shark bearing straight down on me. I shouted for help, and the next moment found myself falling down a well with the shark, an enormous white shark, in full pursuit of me. On arriving at the bottom, I was abruptly transferred to the drawing-room of a house I had not visited or thought of for at least twenty years, when the first thing I saw on the tea-table, its baleful eyes fixed on mine with a malicious grin, was the head of the shark. I awoke in fear and trembling—as indeed I might after such a startling exhibition—and, on coming down to breakfast, learned of the death of a very dear friend.

On another occasion, a day or two before I heard of the death of an old schoolfellow of mine, I dreamed I was fishing in a deep pool overgrown with rushes, when the first thing I caught—or at least which caught me, for I was eventually eaten by it—was a leviathan shark. I can see it now—a huge, slimy, blue-backed thing with a glistening white belly, eyes twinkling with devilish glee at the prospect of so sure a meal, and an enormous, gaping mouth furnished with what seemed to me interminable rows of saw-edged teeth. Snap, in I went, and the next instant the most frightful, the most excruciating agonies shot through me as a thousand spike-like points crushed into my flesh. For some seconds after I awoke I still felt a hellish pain in my eyes, and ears, and all the most sensitive parts of my body.

A lady once told me that the night before hearing of the unexpected promotion of her son, she dreamed she saw him standing in a pool of water literally surrounded by huge salmon, that rubbed themselves affectionately against his legs in the manner of a dog.

And another dream, that has been told me relative to the same fish, was to the effect that shortly before the dreamer received a high official appointment in the East Indies, he dreamed he was paddling in a brook, when he suddenly trod on a huge salmon; that leaped out of the water and went on rising and rising in the air, till it finally disappeared altogether.

It is no uncommon thing for me to dream about eels, and whenever I do, something unpleasant is sure to follow. Either someone plays me a nasty trick, or I lose a train, or catch a cold, or meet with a rebuff; and this, I find, has been the experience of crowds of other people.

FOXES

Foxes figure so largely in folk-lore that one need not be surprised that fox-dreams, in the case of many people, are particularly significant. Silver foxes in dreams would appear to portend excessive good fortune; black foxes, excessive misfortune; ordinary foxes, good luck in a moderate degree.

Among the fox-dreams that have been related to me was one dreamed by a negro. "I dreamed," he said, "I was starving to death in the streets of a big city, and had come to the decision that, sooner than go on in misery, I would terminate my existence in a deep, brown river that flowed sluggishly by me, when suddenly a white fox came bounding down the street, and, stopping in front of me, vomited sovereign after sovereign. With a wild shout of delight, I sprang forward, and, clutching hold of the gold, was filling my pockets with it when I awoke. That day, I found myself the proud possessor of some hundreds of pounds I won in a lottery; but I attributed it all to the fox."

Another man dreamed he was flying a kite, when

his coat-tails were violently pulled, and, on looking round, he saw a white fox that darted swiftly between his legs, and was suddenly metamorphosed into his uncle. The shock was so great that he awoke, and, a day or two later, heard the very same uncle he had seen in his sleep had died and left him his entire fortune.

FROGS

To dream of frogs signifies the advent of domestic trouble, breakages, and petty losses.

HORSES

To dream of white horses foretokens good luck of various kinds; of black horses, serious misfortune in the shape of accidents (frequently on the water), deaths, loss of money or property, violent quarrels and rupture in love affairs; of roan-coloured horses, journeys; of grey horses, good fortune in many forms, viz.: legacies, presents, success in love affairs and work, &c.; of brown horses, nothing in particular; of chestnut horses, danger of all sorts, from fire, water, and other accidents, from assaults, and from illness. To quote even half the horse-dreams that have been told me would fill a book, so I must content myself with merely quoting a few. Shortly before a violent rupture with her husband, which terminated in a divorce, one lady I met told me she had dreamed she heard a loud neighing outside her house, and, on looking out of the window, saw a gigantic black horse, with intensely evil eyes, gazing up at her. Greatly terrified, she turned to run downstairs to see that all the gates were shut, when, to her horror, the horse stalked into the room and rushed savagely at her. She then awoke, and was too frightened to sleep again till the morning.

Another curious dream befell a gentleman I met in Liverpool. Shortly before his house caught on fire and was all but burned to the ground, he dreamed he was cycling along a hot and dry country road, when a chestnut horse appeared upon the scene, and commenced to plunge and shy immediately in front of him. Much alarmed, he got off his bicycle, and was preparing to seek the shelter of a garden he now observed for the first time, close at hand, when the horse rushed at him, and, seizing him viciously by the back, threw him on the ground, and was about to stamp on him when he awoke.

Of a pleasanter nature, was a dream I once had, prior to receiving the welcome tidings of the sale of a manuscript. I dreamed I was toiling painfully along a dusty road, when a beautiful grey horse suddenly trotted up to me; and, with the gentlest expression imaginable in its fine dark eyes, bid me mount. Not in the slightest degree surprised at hearing it speak, I climbed on its back, and the next moment found myself flying through the air. I forget exactly how the dream terminated, but I fancy it was in some remarkably pleasant manner, and that the horse landed me in a floral Elysium, where I fell head over ears in love with a gorgeously apparelled houri.

Then, too, I have dreamed of a roan horse; of seeing it struggling desperately to extricate itself from a morass, till gradually sinking and sinking it disappeared out of sight; and nothing was left to mark the spot where it had vanished but a hideous black bubble. I dreamed this before travelling quite unexpectedly from Bristol to Scotland.

INSECTS

ANTS

Ants in dreams signify presents.

BEES

Bees in dreams foretell good fortune; very often in love affairs, work, or money. Prior to inheriting an unexpected fortune; I have known instances where people have dreamed of swarms of bees buzzing around them; and I well recollect, before my engagement; dreaming I saw myriads of bees trying to get in at my bedroom window. It was a beautiful sight; for their wings and the yellow markings of their bodies sparkled and flashed in the rays of a typical dreamland sun.

BEETLES

To dream of black beetles signifies impending illness, sometimes serious, sometimes slight. Before being laid up with bronchial colds, I very often have very harrowing dreams of being visited by shoals of black beetles and cockroaches.

BUTTERFLIES

Generally speaking, butterfly-dreams are lucky, and signify unexpected good fortune and happiness.

CATERPILLARS

To dream about caterpillars foretells small accidents, such as cuts on fingers, bumps and bruises; and minor ailments, such as colds, neuralgia, toothache.

CENTIPEDES

Centipedes in dreams denote losses—not infrequently the loss of some pet animal or treasure.

DRAGON-FLIES

To dream of dragon-flies presages quarrels, bothers, and unpleasant missions.

EARWIGS

To dream about earwigs foretells danger from an enemy—an enemy who, metaphorically speaking, intends stabbing the dreamer in the back; also, danger from scandal and malicious gossip.

GNATS

Gnats in dreams would seem to have especial significance to the young, as they often signify impending kisses.

LADYBIRDS

Lady-birds in dreams are lucky, and signify presents—often presents from lovers.

MAGGOTS

Maggots in dreams are, as one would suppose, of bad omen; and portend illness, death, quarrels, and losses.

MOTHS

To dream about moths is unlucky, and presages disappointments of all kinds—in money matters, love affairs, and work.

SLUGS

Slugs in dreams foretell jealousy.

SPIDERS

To dream about spiders (with the exception of big black spiders) in general—for there are, of course, many species of this insect—is lucky. It foretells presents; and unexpected success in work and business; also journeys. Black spiders in dreams signify danger from drowning, and falls.

SNAILS

Snails in dreams presage weddings, the reunion of friends, and favourable business transactions.

WASPS

Wasps in dreams foretell pecuniary losses, quarrels and disappointments.

WORMS

Worms in dreams are interpretative of the constancy of lovers and friends; and of recovery from illness, and success on the stage.

KANGAROOS

Kangaroos signify journeys.

LIONS

Lions in dreams portend marriages; success of all kinds, viz.: in love, work, and sport; and unexpected journeys.

Prior to a voyage to the West Indies, planned on the spur of the moment, a lady once told me she dreamed she was crossing the road opposite the house when, on glancing up, she perceived, to her terror, the face of a lion glaring down at her from the nursery window. In an agony of fear for her children's safety, she turned to seek the aid of a man with a gun, when, with a tremendous roar, the lion leaped down and dashed after her—a proceeding which awoke her.

I recollect, too, dreaming I was eaten by a lion, shortly before I made up my mind to go to Oregon, in the summer of 1894.

LEOPARDS, PUMAS AND PANTHERS

These animals in dreams signify violent accidents, serious illness, and death.

MONKEYS

Generally speaking—that is to say, without going into details with regard to species—monkeys in dreams foretell quarrels, the breaking off of engagements, and legal disputes.

MICE

Whereas in some cases mice-dreams would appear to import nothing in particular, in others they undoubtedly point to illness, and death. I remember one lady telling me she had several times dreamed she was surrounded by mice, and that on each occasion the dream was followed by the illness of one of her children.

Another case, in which the mouse-dream foretold illness, is that of a lady who dreamed that she was at a dance one night, and as she was about to commence waltzing a mouse suddenly leaped from off her partner's head on to her own, and bit her on the ear in the most vicious manner. She awoke smarting with the pain and, a few days later, was laid up with a severe attack of influenza. The dream had been so vivid that she could not help remembering it, and associating it in some way with her sickness.

And to quote a case in which the mice-dream foretold death, a lady I once met dreamed that, on going to bed one night, she saw a succession of mice, in Indian file, run across her dressing-table; and on the following morning, she heard one of her brothers had been drowned at sea.

PIGS

Dreams about pigs are decidedly unlucky, and mean anything from slight accidents to downright calamities.

One lady, prior to her youngest child falling down a well and nearly being drowned, dreamed she saw him riding up and down the front lawn on a big white pig, which eyed her with an expression of fiendish malignancy; whilst some one else, shortly before he lost all his money in a brewery, dreamed that he saw a herd of white pigs outside his front door, pawing the ground and uttering the most piteous cries.

RATS

Rats, whether white, black, or brown, singly or collectively, import illness, death, and serious misfortunes.

The night before his son was drowned at sea, a man I once met dreamed his bedroom was full of enormous black rats with grey eyes, that raced round and round the bed, and eventually leaped into the empty grate and disappeared up the chimney.

Another person, a lady in London, if I remember rightly, dreamed that she saw her youngest daughter sitting on the floor playing with a big brown rat that suddenly sprang at her, tore the ribbon out of her hand, and raced out of the room with it. Some days later, this particular daughter developed consumption, of which she eventually died.

SNAKES

Snake-dreams are unlucky, and signify injuries by enemies, scandal, unkind gossip, and falseness on the part of those who have hitherto posed as friends.

From among the many snake-dreams I have heard and recollect, I select the following, as examples.

A lady, who had formed a great friendship with a woman with a peculiar cast in her eyes (a disfigurement which, in my opinion, frequently points to deceit), once dreamed she was walking in her garden, when out of a rose glided an enormous green snake. Greatly alarmed, she was on the verge of running away to solicit help to kill the brute, when she saw, to her amazement, that it had human eyes, and, on bending down to examine it more closely, she found herself looking into the countenance of her woman friend. Hair, features and complexion were exactly similar, but the expression was different: it was an expression of the utmost craftiness and malice, of which she had never for one moment thought her friend capable. She awoke much impressed, and, before the day was out, learned that this very friend had done her the greatest possible injury by betraying a secret of the utmost consequence.

My second illustration is the experience of a man who dreamed he was groping about on the rockery in his garden, when he found, to his horror, a nest of brown snakes, that rose on end and hissed at him. He tried to draw back, but found himself wedged in by a well that had in some mysterious fashion, only to be met with in dreams, suddenly sprung up behind him. Every avenue of escape was closed, and wherever he looked he saw snakes—the wall and the rockery were covered with them. Overcome with terror, he forced himself to wake, and rather than go to sleep again, and risk a continuation or repetition of his dream, he lit the gas and read till morning. The dreamer, shortly afterwards, sustained a pecuniary loss through an act of treachery.

SHEEP

Sheep in dreams imply the advent of trouble in the form of family disputes and disagreements, quarrels with friends and neighbours.

Apart from the experiences of those whom I have met, on which I have based the above statements, I have invariably found that after dreaming of sheep myself I have had to encounter much petty and uncalled-for disagreeableness.

RAMS

Rams in dreams denote quarrels of a more violent nature than do sheep. For example, I remember, when I was a boy, prior to a quarrel (which ended in a fight) with a schoolfellow, dreaming I was attacked in a field by a big black ram with red eyes, that chased me persistently over hedges and ditches, and through water, and when, in some miraculous fashion, I took to the air, it sprang up after me, never desisting from its fierce buttings till I was reduced to a hopeless state of jelly, when I was permitted to awake. In after years, before quarrelling with a venomous attorney, I dreamed I was fishing in a weir, when a grey ram, catching me unawares, butted me in the back and precipitated me head first into the water, where I found myself attacked on all sides by slimy, yellow snakes.

STAGS

Stags in dreams indicate a change in one's life, as, for instance, prior to deciding to migrate as a farmer to Canada, a bank clerk dreamed he was walking through a park, when a beautifully marked stag came bounding up to him, and lifting him up with its antlers, in such a manner as to cause him no inconvenience, whirled him away o'er bank and brae, till it finally arrived on the margin of a silvery sea, where it turned into a yacht and swiftly sailed away.

Another stag-dream some one told me was to the effect that a man, before changing from a parson to an actor, dreamed a white stag appeared by his bedside, and, picking him up in its mouth, sank through the floor into a cabbage-field, where it engaged in a deadly combat with another stag, and, after running the latter through with its horns, was advancing furiously upon the dreamer, when he awoke.

TIGERS

To dream of a tiger signifies the advent of an illness, loss of money, accident, and disappointment in love. For my own part, I dreamed I was stalked and pounced upon by a white tiger, prior to being thrown from a bicycle; whilst a night or two before I was seized with appendicitis—*i.e.* in December 1906—I dreamed a tiger got into the house through one of the lower windows, and after gorging itself on a dog, whose screams half frightened me out of my senses, came stealing up the stairs to attack me. The agonies I underwent, as I heard it drawing nearer and nearer, were such as one could only experience in sleep. I awoke as its hideous, striped head and malevolent, yellow eyes peeped gloatingly in at me through the door.

WOLVES

To dream of wolves signifies some great impending trouble, often financial, sometimes domestic, as, for instance, divorce or separation.

A man once told me that, prior to the discovery of his wife's faithlessness, he dreamed he saw her riding on the back of a huge grey wolf, whilst a white wolf, which she was patting affectionately, trotted by her side. And again, shortly before losing his entire fortune, a man told me he had dreamed a pack of black wolves rushed across his garden, howling in the most hideous manner conceivable, and snapping and tearing at everything that came in their way.

Another man informed me that, just before his daughter ran away from home, he dreamed a big grey wolf leaped into his room and tried to eat him.

Addenda to Animal Dreams

ELEPHANTS

Elephants in dreams signify shipwrecks, marriages, and births.

TOADS

Toads in dreams foretell vicious acts that will either be done to the dreamer or by him.

FLIES

Flies in dreams signify impending illness, generally of a mental nature, and misfortunes of various kinds. For example, a man whom I met abroad told me that he continually dreamed he was tormented with flies, prior to an attack of temporary insanity.

Again, shortly before her children were attacked with scarlet fever, a lady dreamed her room was inundated with green flies; whilst some one else informed me that before losing her billet in an office she dreamed she was bitten on the lip by a blue-bottle, and the pain was so real that, on awakening, she examined the spot to see if there were marks to show that she really had been bitten.

CHAPTER II

ACCIDENTS

To dream of accidents on land (apart from railway accidents) signify reconciliation between relations and friends, and presents in the form of dress.

BIRTHS

To dream of a birth signifies a death. One afternoon, at a garden-party, I met an old friend, who told me he had just dreamed his sister had had a child, and as he was curious to know whether that event had actually occurred, he was going to write at once. The dream was verified, but in a manner he did not anticipate; for, on arriving at his house he found a telegram awaiting him there to say his sister was dead! And again, at a cricket match one baking hot day in July I was speaking of dreams, when one of the players exclaimed with a shudder: "I fear your interpretation of the birth-dream is only too correct. A lady once told my wife that she dreamed she had given birth to a remarkably fine boy, whose eyes, however, were not both of the same colour. Two hours later this lady was run over by a motor and killed!"

BALLOONS

To dream of airships and balloons signifies surprises—surprises of all sorts; also trouble with the eyes and ears.

BRIDGES

To dream of crossing over, or standing on, a bridge signifies a change in the routine of one's life, such as the moving from one house or town to another, or the changing of one's occupation, It also presages sorrow, generally at the loss of a friend.

VIVID COLOURS IN DREAMS

Without going into detail with regard to variety in shade, colour in dreams, especially when it is vivid and predominant, has much significance. The separate meaning of each separate colour in dreams is as follows:

Light blue signifies impending trouble, particularly matrimonial and domestic troubles; serious quarrels between husband and wife, and parents and children; also suicide and murder.

Dark blue, recovery from illness; reconciliation of husband and wife, relatives and friends; presents of animals.

Brown, success in work and business.

Black, illness; and death.

Green, success in anything appertaining to the arts; also an impending visit from an occult presence.

Gold, success in speculation, commerce, and courtship.

Grey, trouble and even danger from unsuspected quarters.

Mauve, death; and violent catastrophe, not infrequently with regard to the sight.

Orange, illness; treachery.

Pink, a wedding or engagement.

Purple, accidents, more particularly on land.

Red, quarrels, voyages, great changes; and accidents, chiefly by fire.

Violet, success in the arts—viz. painting, music, literature.

Yellow, treachery on the part of a friend; act of ingratitude and jealousy.

White, deaths.

Examples. A lady who is intensely psychic, prior to the death of her husband dreamed the bedroom suddenly became black, and that a huge black lobster slowly descended from the ceiling and settled on her. Another lady, whom I have met in literary circles, shortly before her first manuscript was accepted, dreamed that on all the fingers of her right hand she saw rings set with enormous emeralds, and that the sky, stars, and moon were all of the brightest and most vivid green. Prior to going on a quite unexpected trip to America, a man I met dreamed a red pocket handkerchief fluttered through the air and fell on his lap, and when he put out his hand to pick it up, each of his knuckles emitted a lurid scarlet glow. Lastly, prior to a piece of base deception on the part of one who had always posed as her friend, a lady I knew well as a child dreamed she saw a boy walking in front of her with bright yellow hair, and clad from head to foot in the most startling yellow clothes.

DANCING

To dream of dancing with any one in particular signifies that person is contemplating doing you an injury; if your partner be your sweetheart or lover, then the dream is intended to prove he, or she, is inconstant and has been carrying on a flirtation with some one else. If you dream you are dancing by yourself, or you are merely a spectator at a dance, or you are dancing in a crowd of complete strangers, or with a stranger, then the dream portends trouble, usually of a domestic and petty nature.

DEATHS, CORPSES AND FUNERALS

If you dream of a corpse, a death, or a funeral, you will hear of a birth, engagement, or marriage; but not necessarily in connection with the person you dream about. Occasionally, however, the dream is literally verified and the person dreamed about dies. I recollect dreaming I went into the dining-room of a house in which I was staying, and saw on the table a coffin. Horrified out of my senses at so ghastly a spectacle, I would have fled at once, had I not been compelled by an irresistible curiosity to go up to the coffin and peer in. My terror then was inconceivable, for the body I saw was that of my host, his face marred with all the horrible disfigurements of advanced decomposition. But the climax of horror was not yet reached, for, as I gazed, the corpse slowly opened its eyes, and, with a hideous flippancy, winked and leered at me. I awoke sweating with fright, and two or three days later my host died in a fit of apoplexy.

A friend of mine, before the death of her brother,

dreamed she went to the window one still and moonlight night, and, on peeping out, saw her brother standing on the garden path, looking up at her. His eyes were glassy, his cheeks white and fleshless, and he was swathed all over in a winding-sheet. The sight so shocked her that she awoke, and within the week received tidings that her brother was dead. But these are exceptions, and I maintain that as a rule dreams of the dead presage births, engagements, and marriages.

DIGGING

To dream one is digging portends the illness, sometimes the death, of the dreamer ; to dream one sees some one else digging signifies an illness or death, but not necessarily of the digger.

DRESS

To dream of a wedding-dress or winding-sheet portends a death, but not necessarily that of the person directly associated in the dream with the wedding-dress or winding-sheet. To dream of clothes in general signifies petty disappointments and minor ailments.

DRINKING

To dream of drinking portends a visit to a place of entertainment.

DROWNING

To dream one is drowning presages trouble, either domestic or financial, for the dreamer. To see some one else drowning portends misfortune, either from accidents (sometimes drowning, as actually seen in the vision), illness, or loss of money, but not always for the drowning person.

This dream, I find, is a very common one. I have often seen in dreams friends of mine struggling desperately in some deep pool or river. Frantically I have plunged in to their rescue, but always too late, and, on sinking down, down, down, have at length come in contact with their cold, clammy corpses. Quite recently I dreamed I saw a near and dear friend fall shrieking into a seething, hissing pool of muddy water. In an agony of mind I tried to go to his rescue, but was held back by one of those cruel, invisible forces that ever haunt dreams. Desperately I struggled, but with no avail; and all the while I watched the ghastly, hideous terror in my friend's upturned eyes and the increasing pallor in his cheeks. I saw him clutch and unclutch his fingers as he threw them wildly above his head and clawed the air; and then I beheld him sink—sink with one final, blood-curdling scream for help that rang and re-rang through my brain as I awoke. The following day, I received a letter from this friend to say that he was in the greatest trouble owing to the illness of his youngest child; the doctors gave no hope of her complete recovery; they had unhesitatingly pronounced her a cripple for life.

Often have I been drowning in dreams. The Thames has claimed my immaterial body times without number, and my frantic death-struggles have aroused the sympathy of scores of limb-tied spectators on Waterloo Bridge and the Embankment. Could anything on the material plane have been more painfully, more awfully realistic? The cold grey stones of the bridge, the swift-flowing water beneath—yes, ever so far beneath, miles beneath, until I took the plunge, and then—how near! A sensation of falling, of being half stifled by a hurricane of air rushing with cyclonic force up my nostrils, and the next moment—icy coldness, terrifying coldness, and down, down, down into a surging blankness, where all is the darkness of despair and death. And after every dream of this description I have experienced trouble—trouble, always trouble.

EATING

To dream of eating portends an accident to the teeth and visit to the dentist.

FALLING

To dream one is falling portends an unexpected visit and an interruption in one's daily routine. Who has not dreamed of falling ? Of stepping over the edge of some mighty cliff or chasm and plunging —with all the sickly, giddy sensation of plunging— down, down, down, until, instead of experiencing the apparently inevitable final crash, one has awakened This curtailed phase of the falling-dream is so ordinary, in fact, that it is generally supposed that one cannot, in falling down an abyss in a dream, actually arrive at the bottom. However, having had a contrary experience myself, I have to my own satisfaction at least proved this belief to be erroneous.

FINDING THINGS

To pick up money in dreams signifies impending petty troubles. How often have some, perhaps many, of us in our dreams seen a sovereign on the pavement, and, on greedily picking it up, seen another, and then others, until the whole street—like Whittington's of yore—seemed paved with gold. And how bitterly disappointed, I venture to think, have most of us been on awakening, to find the golden harvest flown!

The finding of a coffin in a dream portends a death, usually that of a child. To find bones presages illness or death.

FLOWERS

Since each flower, fruit, tree and vegetable in dreams has a specific meaning, and to deal exhaustively with each would fill volumes, I am again beset with the difficulty of limited space. Speaking then as briefly as possible, in my experience to dream of:

Buttercups portends presents and kisses; carnations, weddings; convolvulus, an enemy, intrigues; cornflowers, success in courtship and work; cowslips, petty troubles; daisies, births; daffodils, inconstancy of lovers; dandelions, illness and minor worries; ferns, a journey; foxgloves, presents; honeysuckle, deceit on the part of a friend; ivy, weddings, friendly actions; lilies, engagements, also deaths; mignonette, sorrow at loss of a friend ; pansies, success in any branch of art ; pinks, success in business ; poppies, breaking off an engagement, work or business, losses ; primroses, new friendships ; roses (white), success in courtship and the arts ; roses (yellow), danger from intrigue and jealousy ; roses (pink), engagements, journeys of pleasure, presents ; roses (red), weddings and legacies, falling in love ; sunflowers, accidents (chiefly on land) ; sweet peas, reunion of parted friends and lovers, kisses ; tulips, deaths, journeys to foreign parts ; wallflowers, visits from old friends and to old places.

Addenda

To dream of forget-me-nots portends visits and presents from old friends, new clothes, success in work ; heliotrope, falling in love, visits to places of amusements, meetings with those likely to influence one in after-life ; violets, reciprocation of one's affections, presents from lovers.

If a girl dreams she is given a bunch of violets by her sweetheart, it is a sure thing he is sincere in his protestations of love.

Kisses : To dream of being kissed by any particular person means that person is not to be trusted. If a girl dreams of being kissed by her lover, it may be regarded as a sign he is inconstant.

TREES

The alder in dreams presages travels, chiefly by sea ; unrest in home life and work.

Ash, bad news of all sorts.

Banyan, journeys and surprises.

Beech, disaffection (or going abroad) of friends ; disappointments in general.

Birch, success in work.

Broom, illness, sometimes death.

Brambles, troubles, both domestic and financial.

Cedar, presents of all kinds ; loss (by death) of old friends.

Chestnut, success in courtship, falling in love.

Clematis, reunion of friends and lovers.

Elm, death of a relation, of an old friend ; or loss of employment.

Hawthorn, sickness.

Hazel, success of an extraordinary nature ; recovery from illness ; escape from an accident.

Lilac, new clothes ; present from lover ; unexpected invitations.

Mistletoe, great success in courtship and the arts.

Olive, falling in love ; the forming of new friendships.

Palm, success in work and rise in social life.

Pine, death, illness; and a journey to foreign parts.

Poplar, danger from drowning or falling.

Willow, death of a great friend or near relation; and sorrow due to illness.

Addendum to Trees

To dream of holly portends illness and domestic trouble.

FRUIT AND VEGETABLES

To dream of apples portends quarrels; beans, presents; cabbages, petty losses; carrots, new dresses and clothes; cherries, presents and kisses; gooseberries, domestic quarrels and legal disputes; grapes, the breaking of friendships; pears, births; plums, minor accidents; wheat, success in work and business, legacies and presents; grass, illness, the breaking off of engagements, disappointments in general; barley and oats, journeys and unexpected visits; hay, weddings, holidays and legacies.

FIRES

To dream of a fire sometimes portends a fire, and sometimes danger from drowning; also financial difficulties and legal disputes.

FLYING

The flying-dream is, I believe, more common to people with the psychic faculty and artistic temperament than to others. I have sounded many artists and writers on the subject, and they tell me that they often dream they are flying, but seldom, if ever, with wings. I know the sensation well, for I frequently experience it in dreamland. Maybe, as I am walking along a road, I suddenly feel I can fly. I give a jump, and the next moment am moving through the air, a yard or so from the ground, with both feet close together. It is a most enjoyable sensation, and I am so entranced that I keep saying to myself: "It is real this time. I am not dreaming. I can fly at last." I sometimes fancy I am in a room full of people, who naturally express the greatest incredulity when I tell them I can fly. To substantiate my statement, I then climb on to the table or chair, spring off, and, with both feet together, rise to the ceiling, much to my own gratification and the edification of my audience. Bitter, indeed, is my chagrin when I awake and discover that I am as far off flying as ever. Again, many is the time I have dreamed I have been in a huge, empty house, pursued by some grotesque monstrosity that, after chasing me up endless staircases and along the most blood-curdling corridors, has at length cornered me in a gloomy top attic. All seems hopeless, and I am expecting to be caught every second, when, just as the dreadful creature bounds into the room, I leap on to the window-sill and, with a prodigious bound, spring into space. And then, joy of joys, instead of falling, I find I can fly—fly far away into the distant, boundless heavens where there is nothing to stop me.

I have carefully counted the number of flying-dreams I have had in twelve months, from January 1, 1910, to January 1, 1911, and find they amount to eighteen—truly, a fair percentage! And what happens after them? Generally a surprise visit, or unexpected journey or letter, or unusually heavy correspondence—nothing more serious. But as dreams go, I know of few that are more fascinating.

MADNESS

To dream of madness presages impending trouble of all sorts. Not infrequently the dream is, to a large extent, fulfilled. I well recollect a lady saying to me once: "I dreamed last night that my brother and I were sitting by ourselves in the breakfast-room, when, something making me suddenly look up at him, I perceived a curious glitter in his eyes—a glitter that made my blood run cold. Presently, he made the most frightful grimace, baring his teeth, bulging out his eyes and frowning, and then all his features contorted as if they were india-rubber, and I saw something too evil and repulsive for words. With a shriek of terror I sprang up and made a rush for the door, and as I did so he gave a loud chuckle and bounded after me, crying out: 'I'm mad! I'm mad! Say your prayers, I'm going to chop you to pieces!' I awoke in a dreadful fright, just as he caught me by the hair and was going to kill me. Within a week, I heard that he had softening of the brain and had to be confined in a private home."

MARRIAGE

To dream of a marriage frequently signifies a death or illness, but not necessarily of the bride or bridegroom.

MOON

To dream of the moon portends illness, usually mental, but not necessarily that of the dreamer; also domestic and financial troubles, and death by drowning.

When I was in Cornwall some years ago, I mentioned a boating fatality that had occurred quite recently in the harbour to a local fisherman, who at once exclaimed, "Aye! Aye! I knew something of the sort would happen, for I dreamed of the moon two nights following"; and he then went on to explain, that whenever he had such dreams, somebody was sure to be drowned.

MONEY

To dream of picking up money, as I have already stated, signifies petty troubles. To dream of seeing money, minor ailments and surprise visits.

MURDER

To dream one is being murdered portends domestic troubles, and trouble with neighbours, and losing things. To dream that another person is murdered sometimes signifies great danger to that person—indeed, the dream is occasionally verified—or trouble of some sort to that person, or to some one connected with that person.

For example, I have been told of a lady, who dreamed most vividly that she saw a woman enter her aunt's room, whilst the latter was asleep, and smother her with a pillow. Everything was most realistic—the door slowly opening ; the white-faced, evil-eyed servant with a candle ; her stealthy, gliding footsteps ; her coarse hands, knotted knuckles and broken nails ; the expression of fiendish glee in her eyes as she took up the pillow, and the quick, subtle jerk with which she brought it down on to the sleeper's face ; the tightening of her lips ; the straightening of her bare arms as she pressed on her victim with all her weight ; and the kicking of the bedclothes, at first frantic and then faint, and finally ceasing altogether with one tiny tug at the sheet—when the sleeper awoke. All was most graphic, all most hellish. Some few days later, this lady heard of the death of her aunt. She had been robbed and murdered in a boarding-house in Vienna.

CHAPTER III

THE NAKED-DREAM

Who has not dreamed of being suddenly bereft of their clothes and of finding themselves in some public place, the cynosure of all eyes, without even so much as a pocket-handkerchief? A dream of this kind happened to some one I know—some one who is much to the fore in society. He dreamed that he and his brother were strutting up and down Bond Street, when he suddenly noticed that every one was looking at them in a very odd and marked manner. Wondering what it could mean, he hurriedly glanced at his person (the subject of clothes, by the way, was ever uppermost in his mind), and, to his undying shame and horror, saw that he was naked, and so was his brother. In an agony of mind, he caught hold of the latter by the arm and whispered: "For goodness sake, Dick, make for the first cab you see! And don't stop to ask questions!" But his brother shook him off. "How ridiculous! I shall do nothing of the sort!" he said. "I came here to walk, and walk I shall. Ah! By Jove! there is Mrs. So-and-so. How well she looks!" and in the most gallant manner possible he took off his hat and bowed. A universal shriek was the result, and a piping voice—that of the charming girl's small brother—was heard to cry out, "Look, look, Ethel! There are the De Jones, and they have nothing on!" Then a huge policeman bounced across the road, and in a moment the two brothers were hustled along the busy thoroughfare, with half London at their heels. I cannot remember what my friend told me happened to him next, but I well remember him assuring me that, until he woke up, he certainly had an exceedingly disagreeable time of it. The dream, however, foretold good fortune; for my friend, who was in the army, received unexpected promotion shortly afterwards.

In one instance my own experience of the naked dream was very similar. In this dream I went to a fancy dress ball attired, as I thought, in some very fantastic but complete costume of the Middle Ages. To my surprise, however, the moment I entered the ballroom there was a loud chorus of "Oh's!" and every one stopped dancing to stare at me. Feeling rather flattered than otherwise, I was making my way to one of the only available seats, when the host, his face aglow with fury, strode across the room, and, in a voice quivering with passion, said, "How dare you, sir! How dare you disgrace yourself and me by coming to my ball like this?" Thoroughly taken aback, I replied that I did not know there was anything so very out of the way in my choice of costume. "Indeed," I stammered, "I think it most ordinary." "Altogether too ordinary! Too infernally ordinary!" thundered my host. "Look at yourself in that glass!" and he pointed to a huge mirror as he spoke. Then my blood turned to ice. I had—yes, I had come as Adam—Adam before the Fall! "Chase him!" shrieked my host, "Chase the insolent wretch, and when you catch him, skin him alive!" Hardly were the words. out of his mouth before the guests and musicians, armed with chairs, fans, and violins, rushed, shrieking and yelling, at me; but, happily for me, I was still some few feet ahead of my pursuers, when I awoke.

On another occasion, I dreamed I was handing round the bag in some fashionable church, when all the men suddenly turned round and scowled at me, and the ladies fainted. Utterly unable to conceive what I had done, I was about to sneak away as fast as I could, when the verger suddenly tapped me on the shoulder and, in a stage whisper, said, "I beg pardon, sir, I don't want to say anything disrespectful, but what has become of your clothes? You had them on right enough a moment ago." To my unmitigated dismay, I now perceived that what the verger said was only too true—my clothes, *in toto*, had been taken from me; I was absolutely and shamelessly nude. With a howl of anguish, I dropped the bag and awoke.

Immediately after each of these dreams I experienced unexpected success in my work.

From what I have been told, I conclude that it is the more prudish and ostentatiously pious people who are the more often subjected to this kind of dream. I remember once travelling on board a steamer with a Nonconformist minister as the sharer of my cabin. In all respects he was of the middle class, middlish—being supercilious and smug, and of course very respectable—at least, respectable in all but his dreams, which he narrated to me with so obvious a relish for detail, that I could not help thinking he enjoyed them rather than otherwise.

"It is a sure sign I am a very good man," he said to me on one occasion, "because I am being tempted continually in my sleep. Were I not good, the devil would not have to resort to so subtle a device to seduce me. Last night I dreamed I was calling on some of my most highly respected parishioners—the Gardners. Mr. Gardner (it was one of the minister's idiosyncrasies to bore me to death with the family histories of all his congregation) is a grocer in Lemon Street, and must be making a good six hundred a year clear profit. He hires a carriage every Sunday afternoon—not that I approve of desecrating the Sabbath in such a manner—only in his case there is some excuse, as he is hard-working and honest, and his wife is too delicate to walk; she is most genteel, she invariably dresses in silk when she comes to chapel, and gives most liberally. Her daughter's name is Martha—Martha!" and he turned up his eyes heavenwards as he repeated the name. "Well, to prove to you how sorely the devil tries me," he went on, "I dreamed last night I was calling on the Gardners, and, just as Mrs. Gardner was handing me a cup of tea, into the room, with a bounce and giggle (so utterly unlike herself; she is a most decorous young woman), came Martha — Martha wearing one of those short skirts so popular with the depraved aristocracy, and her feet—bare!"

"Only her feet?" I exclaimed. "Was that all?"

"All!" my companion sighed reproachfully—"all! And was not that enough, and more than enough? Bare feet! Oh, how indecent! But I can assure you, much though the devil tempted me, I did not look twice at them. I kept my eyes glued to my cup. And her mother—her mother! oh, how shocked she was! 'Martha!' she screamed, clutching hold of me for support, 'Martha! Are you bereft of your senses? Whatever has come over you? And before Mr. Simpson, of all people! What mortification!' 'Well, ma, neither of you need talk!' Martha retorted, her face one broad, shameless grin. 'Neither need pa, for he is dealing out the groceries in just the same plight. Oh, what a day we're having!' But, before she had finished, Mrs. Gardner (don't ask me to describe *her*) had fled from the room with a shriek; and I, catching sight of myself in the mirror, had all but fainted. I was nude—quite nude—absolutely and wickedly nude!"

"Well, cheer up!" I ejaculated, "for you have got plenty on now, at any rate"—which was only too true, for Mr. Simpson was one of those people who, not content with excluding the fresh air, only partly undress at night and go to sleep in more than half the clothes they have been wearing in the daytime. On our arrival in port he received the welcome news—which he certainly lost no time in making public—that he had been promoted to another and more lucrative living.

Dreams of this sort generally augur well.

HANGING

To dream one is going to be hanged, or to see some one else hanged, portends violent quarrels between relatives and friends, separation and divorce.

PEOPLE OF A CERTAIN PROFESSION OR TRADE

To dream of an actor or actress portends success in courtship; an author, a *rencontre* with an old friend; a baker, missing a train; a builder, a present in the way of dress; a clergyman, neuralgia or biliousness; a coachman, an injury to the head; a chemist, getting into debt; a dentist, illness or death; a dressmaker, kisses; a doctor, danger from cows and horses; a gardener, an accident to the feet or legs; a grocer, sickness; a lawyer, pecuniary losses and danger from dog-bites; a manicurist, presents from a lover, success in courtship; a parvenu, danger from tramps; a publisher, danger from stinging; a member of Parliament, a birth; a sailor, an accident to a clock or watch; a soldier, breaking china or glass; a tailor, quarrel with parents-in-law; a tinker, visit from mother-in-law, or debts incurred by wife or sweetheart ; a tramp, present of a dog or cat ; an undertaker, danger from loose or decayed teeth.

PRESENTS

To dream of presents signifies coming losses usually of no great significance.

RAGS

Rags in a dream portend a fortune.

SLEEP

To dream one is asleep presages a visit from, or to, an old friend.

THE SUN

To dream of the sun portends success in business and distinction in work.

Addenda

The significance of stones (precious and otherwise). Amethyst, success in courtship ; bloodstones, legacies ; coral, a birth ; cornelian, treachery ; diamonds, drowning ; emeralds, great success in the arts ; jasper, inconstancy ; opal, separation, divorce, rupture in friendships; pearls, great sorrow; rubies, lover's kisses; turquoise, the breaking off of an engagement; sapphires, a wedding; common pebbles, petty troubles; black rocks, illness and death; sand, a serious calamity; chalk, ailment or death of a child; granite, accident on land; marble, death.

To dream of teeth coming out portends illness or death, but not necessarily of the dreamer. For example, a man told me that, on the night preceding the death of one of his brothers, he dreamed his teeth fell out, and that on one of them was a portrait of the brother who died.

TRAVELLING

To dream of travelling by sea signifies unexpected news, an invitation, a visit from a stranger. To dream of travelling by land portends minor worries and losses.

Who has not dreamed that they have been rushing to the railway station—that they have missed their train, or that they have got into the wrong train, which proved to be a non-stop to goodness knows where? Or that they have got into the train without a ticket, or without their friends, or without their luggage; or that they have seen their friends go sailing away in the wrong train, and they themselves stranded in some strangely unfamiliar and impossible place? Indeed, everything goes wrong in travelling in dreamland, and when we awake with our brain in a swirl, we are for the moment conscious only that we are lost, and that we will never see our home and relatives again. I have gone through all this frightful waste of vital energy, and so have most people. Again, who has not travelled in a ship that, instead of going where she is intended, sulkily decides to go to the bottom, proceeding to do so in the most peremptory and blood-curdling fashion? And here, let me add, that to dream of shipwreck signifies danger from accidents on land, usually minor and trivial; whereas to dream of railway disaster means danger from water as well as from other sources.

SUICIDE

To dream one commits suicide portends illness, and trouble of all kinds. To dream one sees some one else commit suicide also signifies illness and trouble, and the dream is sometimes verified.

WATER

To dream of clear water portends good fortune of various kinds, and the end of trouble ; to dream of muddy water, illness, death, and troubles of all sorts.

WEATHER

To dream of the wind signifies quarrels, the making of an enemy, and trouble in courtship and matrimony. To dream of rain portends tears ; of snow and ice, illness or death ; of sunshine, success in love, legacies and presents.

THE HOTCH-POTCH DREAM

(A RECAPITULATION)

The dreams in which one flies from one scene to another with breathless rapidity, and all the characters are bewilderingly mixed and everything is hopelessly incongruous, though apparently very meaningless, often contain many significant features.

To quote an illustration : A certain Dr. Eastlake dreamed he was cycling through Hyde Park one very sunny morning, when a servant-maid, dressed all in pink and yellow, shot a perambulator straight in front of him, and he was thrown head over heels in the air; but instead of alighting on the ground, he found himself running about in a cage at the Zoo without anything on. Then, just as his mother-in-law, her face green with fury, advanced on him with uplifted parasol, the scene changed, and he was picking up sovereigns in the street as fast as he could. One of the coins, as he was about to pop it into his pocket, turned into his friend Captain Macgregor, who, forcing him under a pump, made him drink and drink till he could hold no more. The captain then produced a Maxim gun, and swore that unless Dr. Eastlake went on drinking he would fire; whereupon the unfortunate dreamer was about to try and squeeze more water down his throat, when the pump was suddenly converted into a steamer, and he found himself struggling desperately to join his wife, who was already seated, and in imminent danger of being crushed to death by a huge baby that had been thrust into the berth, that was too frail to support such a stupendous weight, just over her head. Oh, the agony of that moment!—his beloved wife in the utmost peril of her life, and he frustrated on all sides in his efforts to save her! Just as he had mounted the gunwale of the ship, the steamer hooted, the captain hurled him brutally off, and he saw the berth give way, the baby fall, and his wife's head squash like an egg. Then, swearing and screaming, he tumbled backwards, and was precipitated into the drawing-room of his own house, where he found his wife carrying on a desperate flirtation with the one man he detested more than any one else. The villain had his arm round her waist and was smothering her with kisses, which she returned every now and then with the greatest effusion; and goodness alone knows what might have happened, had not Dr. Eastlake, with shouts of wrath, leaped in through the window and cut off the heads of his wife and her lover with one sweep of his razor. But, to his horror, the man and woman he had killed, far from being the people he imagined them to be, were two of his richest patients who had come to consult him. Whilst he was deliberating what to do, the door burst open, and his wife followed by all her relations dashed in and denounced him, whereupon he was taken to the police-station, and in the bitter rawness of a cold grey morning—hanged!

In this dream, confused and nonsensical as it appears, there are yet many items of significance. The sunshine denotes success in love; the pink and yellow dress of the maid, a wedding and treachery respectively. The accident, reconciliation ; running about in a state of nudity, success in work ; the green in the mother-in-law's face, success in the arts. Picking up money, petty troubles ; water (clear), end of troubles and good fortune again ; travelling by sea, a visit from a stranger and unexpected news. Accident to wife, trouble about a will. Kisses, inconstancy. Murder, domestic troubles. Hanging, divorce.

All these presages were verified thus : Shortly after the dream, Dr. Eastlake proposed to a girl and was accepted. The marriage took place within a very short time, and almost directly after it, the couple quarrelled owing to a statement made to Dr. Eastlake by one of his wife's friends. Reconciliation, however, soon took place, contemporary with which came the news that Dr. Eastlake had obtained a very good appointment in the town, and that his wife's picture had been "hung on the line." After this there were numerous differences between the two, the artistic temperament of Mrs. Eastlake according ill with that of her husband, who was essentially matter-of-fact and practical. There was then another brief spell of happiness. Dr. Eastlake received a totally unexpected visit from a cousin, whom he had not seen since they were boys together, and the day the cousin left he was summoned to the bedside of his dying father. The latter, in his will, left the bulk of his fortune to a stranger who had for a long time been exercising a sinister influence over him, which influence, however, though obviously undue, could not be legally proved. The disappointment with regard to the will led to further troubles with his wife, whose inconstancy was brought home to Dr. Eastlake with such startling conviction that he had no other alternative than to divorce her. Now, since all these things happened in rapid succession, it is quite clear to my mind that, despite its apparent absurdity the hotch-potch dream may mean much that is tragic.

SUMMARY FOR LOVERS

To dream the object of one's affections is clothed in light blue or yellow signifies they are fickle; in dark blue or gold, that they are constant. To present to or receive from the object of one's affections, or to see him or her wearing a convolvulus, yellow rose, poppy, or daffodil means he or she is inconstant. On the other hand, if in the place of these flowers are buttercups, white roses, or sweet peas, it means he or she is true. To dream one is kissing one's sweetheart portends inconstancy on the part of the dreamer; to dream one sees one's sweetheart kissing, or being kissed, by some one else, foretells the inconstancy of the one dreamed about: To dream one is dancing with the object of one's affection means that the latter is, or will be, guilty of carrying on a flirtation with some one else. To dream of the object of one's affections in connection with ash or beech trees, grass, crows, owls, tortoiseshell cats, spaniels, eels, black horses, earwigs, moths, monkeys, wasps, tigers, wolves, and hanging, signifies fickleness and inconstancy on the loved one's part, which not infrequently leads to a breaking off of the engagement, and, in cases of marriage, to separation and divorce.

To dream of one's beloved one in connection with cherries, ducks, and gnats portends kisses from him or her ; to dream of him or her in connection with cedars, lilacs, pigeons, and ladybirds portends presents ; to dream of him or her in connection with clematis, black cats, silver foxes, grey horses, bees, worms, and lions signifies he or she is constant, that the engagement will lead to marriage, and that the latter will prove in every way happy.

PART II

OUT OF THE ORDINARY DREAMS

CHAPTER IV

DREAMS OF THE AFFLICTED

I HAVE often questioned those who have been born blind as to their dreams. They can, of course, only judge of dreamland by the impression it conveys to their senses of smell, hearing and feeling. One blind man, a musician, told me he had most of the ordinary dreams, such as those of falling, flying, and drowning. "But," he added, "my most common dream is to imagine I can see, and when I awake and find I am still blind, totally blind, the disillusion is most cruel. I invariably have this dream before a severe cold in my head. Before financial worries, I have dreamed I am being chased from room to room in a big, empty castle by something that is not a human being, something I have never met in real life but which I can only presume must be a ghost. I cannot describe it, saving that it brings with it a very peculiar atmosphere that suggests to my mind an extremely cold, bizarre, and antagonistic presence. It fills me with the most fearful terror, and I awake trembling from head to foot."

Another blind man told me that, before an illness or death, he invariably dreamed he lost his way out-of-doors, and eventually found himself in a street where everyone was singing and dancing, and that, on his arrival, they joined hands and danced round him in a circle, and would not let him escape, till, for very weariness he sank on the ground, when all became silent and cold as the grave and he awoke shaking with fear.

Another blind man told me that prior to a visit from his brother, he nearly always dreamed he was walking in a field full of blind animals, that surrounded him on all sides, and felt him all over with their paws. They then suddenly vanished, and he found himself knee deep in water, when he invariably awoke.

I once met a blind woman who informed me that, prior to receiving any disappointment, she always dreamed she was tormented by a little boy with a square-shaped head, who bit and pinched her till she shrieked with pain, when someone instantly came running up and shot him, and she always awoke with the report of the gun ringing in her ears.

The ordinary dreams, such as I have mentioned in Part I, would seem to have the same significance to the blind as to other people.

THE DEAF AND DUMB

"What is my most common dream?" a man who was born deaf and dumb wrote, in answer to my question, "Why! I cannot say offhand, but I believe the dream I am trying to catch a train and cannot make any of the railway officials understand me. I can't say I dream it before any very unusual occurrence, though it is often prior to some slight domestic bother. Yes! I dream of falling, not flying, drowning, picking up money, and many of the other things you mention, and they have precisely the same significance. I dream, too, I can speak with my mouth, and that, usually, before an illness, such as a severe cold or sickness. I think my most alarming dream is when I fancy I am blind, the agony I endure is, then, something frightful, and I awake crying bitterly. I have had this dream before hearing of a death."

IDIOTS

To extract any definite information from an idiot as to his dreams is next to impossible, and after many and sundry vain efforts I have had to desist. From what I have been told, however, by one who had charge of an idiot, the latter used very often to dream he was being chased by something alarming, that he was in danger of being drowned, and that he had all his toys taken from him. The idiot was often ill after the drowning dream, and very fretful and bad-tempered after dreaming he had lost his toys. The grimaces and noises he made in his sleep were generally more *outré* than those he made when awake—often, indeed, most terrifying. Once, and that a day or two before he had an accident, he evidently dreamed he was flying, for he sat up in bed and flapped his arms up and down, emitting, as he did so, an odd crooning sound.

THE INSANE

Mad people, I fancy, often dream of the subject of their mania. One madman, I was told, who believed he was a teapot, used constantly to dream that he was pouring out tea, and when anything prevented the tea flowing he would, on awaking, conclude it was a bad omen, and declare he was going to be ill; which prediction not infrequently came true. Another madman used often to tumble out of bed with a loud bump, and, on being questioned about it by his keeper, would say: "I can't help it; I'm a plum, and when I dream I am ripe I am bound to fall." This same man declared that whenever he dreamed he was eaten, something bad would always happen to him next day.

I once heard of a mad woman who believed she was John the Baptist, and said that, whenever she dreamed she was in the wilderness and the figs were too green to eat, she heard bad news of her friends and relatives. As far as I can gather, insane people often have dreams similar to those of the sane, and, in some instances at all events, they are followed by similar results.

MURDERERS

Murderers, I understand, often re-enact their crimes in their sleep, and have not infrequently been caught owing to their inability to avoid visiting the scene of the tragedy, which has been depicted with such fascinating vividness in their dreams. One murderer, I was told, the day before he was hanged, dreamed he was married and that his bride was the person he had so barbarously murdered for a few shillings.

Though murderers often do have very harrowing dreams the night before their execution, this is by no means invariably the case, as I have heard instances of murderers, on the eve of execution, having enjoyed a sleep in every respect as sound and tranquil as the sleep of the just.

T. Charley, in his *News from the Invisible World*, quotes the following extraordinary instances of warnings of murder in dreams, taken from a work entitled *Records of my Life*, by John Taylor.

"Mr. Fox, in order to attend the House of Commons, had taken an apartment in St. Anne's Churchyard, Westminster. On the evening when he took possession, he was struck with something that appeared to him mysterious in the manner of the maid-servant, who looked like a man disguised, and he felt a very unpleasant emotion. This feeling was strengthened by a similar deportment in the mistress of the house, who soon after entered his room and asked if he wanted anything before he retired to rest. Disliking her manner, he soon dismissed her and went to bed, but the disagreeable impression made on his mind by the maid and the mistress kept him long awake. At length, however, he fell asleep. During his sleep he dreamed that the corpse of a gentleman, who had been murdered, was deposited in the cellar of the house. This dream, co-operating with the unfavourable or rather repulsive countenances and demeanour of the two women, precluded all hopes of renewed sleep ; and it being the summer season, he rose about four o'clock in the morning, took his hat, and resolved to quit a house of such alarm and terror. To his surprise, as he was leaving it, he met the mistress in the entry, dressed as if she had never gone to bed. She seemed to be much agitated, and enquired his reason for wishing to go out so early in the morning. He hesitated a moment with increased alarm, and then told her that he expected a friend, who was to arrive by a stage coach in Bishopsgate Street, and that he was going to meet him. He was suffered to go out of the house, and when revived by the open air he felt, as he afterwards declared, as if relieved from impending destruction. He stated that, in a few hours after, he returned with a friend to whom he had told his dream and the impression made on him by the maid and the mistress. The friend, however, only laughed at him for his superstitious terror ; but on entering the house, they found that it was deserted, and calling a gentleman who was accidentally passing, they all descended to the cellar, and actually found a corpse in the state which the gentleman's dream had represented. Before I make any observations on the subject," Mr. Taylor goes on to say, "I shall introduce a recital of a similar description, and care not if scepticism sneer, or deride, satisfied that I heard it from one on whose veracity I could most confidently depend. (I will, however, now take leave of Mr. Donaldson, though I could with pleasure dwell much longer on the memory of so valuable a friend.) The other extraordinary story to which I have alluded, I heard from what I consider unimpeachable authority. Mrs. Brooke, whom I have already mentioned, told me that she was drinking tea one evening in Fleet Street, when a medical gentleman was expected but did not arrive till late. Apologising for his delay, he said he had attended a lady who suffered from a contracted throat, which occasioned her great difficulty in swallowing. He said she traced the cause to the following circumstance. When she was a young woman, and in bed with her mother, she dreamed that she was on the roof of a church struggling with a man, who attempted to throw her over. He appeared in a carman's frock and had red hair. Her mother ridiculed her terror, and bade her compose herself to sleep again ; but the impression of her dream was so strong that she could not comply. In the evening of the following day,she had appointed to meet her lover at a bowling green, from which he was to conduct her home when the amusement ended. She passed over one field in hopes of meeting the gentleman, and, singing as she tripped along, had entered the second field, when, accidentally turning her head, she beheld in a corner of the field just such a man as her dream represented, dressed in a carman's frock, with red hair, and apparently approaching towards her. Her agitation was so great that she ran with all speed to the stile of the third field and, with difficulty, got over it. Fatigued, however, with running, she sat on the stile to recover herself, and, reflecting that the man might be harmless, she was afraid that her flight might put evil and vindictive thoughts into his head. While she thus meditated, the man had reached the stile, and seizing her by the neck, he dragged her over the stile, and she remembered no more. It appeared that he had pulled off all her clothes and thrown her into an adjoining ditch. Fortunately, a gentleman came to the spot, and observing a body above the water, he hailed others who were approaching, and it was immediately raised. It was evidently not dead, and some of the party remarking that the robber could not be far off went in pursuit of him, leaving others to guard and to endeavour to revive the body. The pursuers went different ways, and some, at no great distance, saw a man sitting at a public-house with a bundle before him. He seemed to be so much alarmed at the sight of the gentlemen, that they suspected him to be the culprit, and determined to examine the bundle, in which they found the dress of the lady, which some of them recognised. The man was, of course, immediately taken into custody, and was to be brought to trial at the approaching assizes. The lady, however, was too ill to come into court, but appearances were so strongly against him that he was kept in close custody. When she was able to give evidence, though he appeared at the trial in a different dress, and with a wig on, she was struck with terror at the sight of him and fainted. On recovering, however, she gave evidence and the culprit was convicted and executed. The medical man added that, when she had finished her narrative, she declared that she felt the pressure of the man's hand on her neck while she related it; and that her throat had actually contracted from the time when the melancholy event occurred."

But these two instances of the murder dream being verified are, of course, exceptions to the general rule, and should any of my readers be so unfortunate as to dream they are being murdered

—I trust that it will only lead, as is usually the case, to trouble of a most ordinary and trivial nature.

ILLNESS

I have always tried to remember the dreams I have had in the delirium of fever and illness, and in many of these dreams there has figured the same woman—clad in black, with long, flowing, black hair, and wild animal eyes—eyes that might have belonged to a woman of the stone age. Thrice, before the deaths of those I have loved, I have dreamed that this same woman has glided up to my bedside and bitten and pinched me. And on each occasion I have awakened with the sting of her sharp, cruel teeth, and her hard, bony fingers burning into my flesh. Can she, I ask myself, be the banshee? But to revert to my deliriums, the deliriums of my youth, in chicken-pox, and measles, and of my later days, in rheumatic fever, dysentery, and severe colds. Apart from this woman in black, who has stood, crouched, sat, or lain at the foot of my bed with greedy expectation in her eyes, I have seen countless other forms and faces; human faces on animal bodies, and vice versa; countenances all awry, and convulsed alternately with anger and merriment; hotch-potches of clothes and limbs mixed anyhow; and yet—yet, despite the apparent chaos, after long and earnest thought I have come to the conclusion that all, all may contain some subtle, hidden meaning. Each contortion of the face, each monstrous feature, each action, gesture, and colour may, and in all probability does, contain its own peculiar significance; interpretative, had I but the key, to the language of the past, the future —and the secrets of the occult world.

The same observation applies to the dreams of the opium smoker—the dreams wherein he travels through scenes of surpassing beauty and strangeness—scenes which rise up before him with extraordinary reality and vividness. And each tableau has its meaning—nay, not merely each tableau, but each item in each tableau—from the quivering of a leaf to the hue of the sky and trees; and trees, flowers, grass, rocks and pebbles, even the glistening of the water, the whispering of the wind, the odours in the atmosphere—all, all contain a whole world of suggestion—of significance. And, yet again, in the fancies of delirium tremens, those wild, frightful fancies of snakes, and rats, and devils, that surround the wretched drunkard on all sides, and twist, and turn, and twirl—some red, some black, some blue—in these too, there may be meaning—each animal, each colour, each gyration each convolution may have its individual purport. Amid the most extravagant confusion there may yet be some slender thread of connection.

CHAPTER V

PHANTASTIC DREAMS

MOST writers and artists live in dreamland. In their hours of wakefulness, Phantasmagoria comes to them; in their hours of sleep they go to Phantasmagoria. Pursued and pursuing, in bed, at work or at play, they are never free from fantasies. In my novels my imagination runs riot, I make no attempt to suppress it. I write of the fantastic the weird, the occult; for at night I move, I breathe, I think in phantom land. So often have I visited this same phantom land that I have made a map of it, naming its isles, seas, mountains; lakes, forests; rivers, and plains. With many of the smaller landmarks, too, I am familiar; and I know what each turn and twist of certain roads have in store for me. Everything is portrayed to me so vividly that I believe my spiritual body, separating itself from my material body, actually visits the superphysical plane and participates in its events. As types of the fantastic dream I quote the following:

DREAM I: A FOREST

Soon after getting into bed one night (in January, 1908), I fell into a deep, blank sleep, from which I was abruptly torn to find myself at the entrance to a forest, a forest I knew, by sight, only too well. It was the forest of Trouble, and, willy-nilly, I had to enter it. On all sides, leviathan trees of the blackest ebony shot up hundreds of feet heavenwards, permitting only the feeblest rays of light to penetrate through their forked branches. What species of trees they were I do not know, for nothing I had seen outside my dreams resembled them. Their trunks were smooth, and in their mirror-like surfaces I could see reflected the workings of their innermost organs, whilst the rising and falling of their hollow voices was wafted down to me from on high, like the murmuring of wind from some mountain top. Nimble hands guided me to a path, and, after setting me in my course, left me to pursue my way as best I could. Plunging irresolutely into the gloom, I followed the winding of the path with considerable uneasiness, fearing to tread lest I should be precipitated into some abyss, and momentarily anticipating the appearance of the strange and uncouth race of people, previous experience had told me inhabited the wood. On and on I went, my fears increasing with the gloom, which, at last, became so impenetrable that I was compelled to halt. I could see nothing, nothing but the faint glimmer of tree trunks; for the rest, all was blackness. I was then suddenly whisked off my feet by a body that shot precipitately between my legs, and, with the wind howling like ten thousand demons through my ears, I was borne through space. For a long period all was turmoil, speed, and darkness; I could feel a thousand objects brush against me, hear the jarring echoes and vibrations of a thousand voices, and then—in one brief instant—all had changed. It was light, a peculiar phosphorous glow pervaded everything, and I found myself in a new plane sitting astride a gigantic beetle with all the trees in the forest running after me. I say "running," for they all had legs, long and spidery legs, and arms too, whilst their stature having considerably decreased, their proportions differed little from that of tall human beings. As they ran they all laughed, a deep mechanical "Ha, ha, ha!" and raising their hands above their heads, they waved them menacingly at me. But the beetle bore me gallantly on, and, despite the desperate efforts the trees made to overtake us, we still maintained our lead. We had progressed a considerable way in this manner, when I suddenly saw, stretched across our track, a white coffin which rose up on end, and shook off its lid, and disclosed to my startled eyes a man, clad from head to foot in red tights. Stepping out from his prison, he placed his fingers in his mouth and whistled shrilly, whereupon the scene once more changed and I found myself back again in the forest, sitting at the foot of a huge, black tree, with the red man opposite me. "You are fond of music?" he said, "then listen!" and placing a flute to his lips, he blew. The most ghastly, the most hellish of noises rang through the forest, and, ere my shocked senses had time to recover I found myself once again in motion—this time on my own legs—with all the trees, headed by the red man, in hot pursuit of me. On and on I tore, till just as I was on the verge of falling, hopelessly dead beat, a vast green sea rose up silently before me, and, stumbling into it, I awoke.

The significance of the vivid colouring in this dream may be interpreted thus: The black of the trees portended illness, which was speedily verified in the long and protracted illness of my wife; the red of the man foretold change, which was verified in my abandoning the scholastic profession for that of the pen; and the green of the sea predicted success in one or other of the arts, which prediction was fulfilled in the success of the book I was then compiling.

Dream II : AN ISLET

I dreamed one night I left my material body, which I saw lying stretched before me on the bed, and that after patting it affectionately on the head; I mounted the window-sill and dived head first into the blackness of the night. Down, down, down I went, the cold air whistling and humming about my ears till I thought the drums would burst. Down, down; eternally down, till all became hushed and silent as the grave, and I perceived to my amazement that the earth was fast disappearing in the distance; and that I was rapidly approaching one of the other planets. Dropping gently, I alighted on a tiny hillock, and discovered I was on an islet that lay in the midst of a sparkling, amethyst ocean. All around me were flowers; pink and white roses, pansies, forget-me-nots, carnations, and many others known only in Dreamland. A breeze, laden with scents suggestive of all the charms of an idyllic summer; made me long to linger there for ever, and, in an ecstacy of delight, I flew from flower to flower, filling my lungs with their soul-inspiring nectar. While engaged in this entrancing pastime, I heard the joyful utterance of a bird, and, on looking up, perceived a lark. With a movement of its little head, which plainly bade me follow; it flew slowly away, and, obeying its injunction I speedily found myself on the banks of a stream where a boat lay moored. Springing into it and taking up the oars, I pushed out into the middle of the current, the lark still continuing to be my guide. The stream, in whose marvellous pellucid depths was reflected the red green of the foliage that lined its shores, took a thousand turns, so that one could never see any great stretch of its gleaming surface at a time, and a very few sweeps of the oars sufficed to shoot my skiff from one angle to another. The character of my surroundings changed as I advanced; the banks and trees grew in height until little of the sky could be seen; the rapidity of the stream ceased, and the waters became deep and tranquil; whilst over and above all hung a silence that brought with it an exquisite sense of rest, intermingled with which was a faint suggestiveness of something bizarre and ghoulish. An unusually abrupt bend, round which the boat subtly glided, laid before me a spectacle so extraordinary that for some seconds I was almost dazed. I had emerged into a gigantic circular basin of several miles in diameter, and entirely composed of glittering white marble. All around it were steps that led down, down, down, until they were lost to sight in the immensity of the distance, the water in some miraculous manner having disappeared altogether. I was deliberating what I had better do, when an enormously tall, nude figure—not unlike a human being—brushed past me, and, turning round, laid one of its long, gleaming fingers against its nose—and smiled knowingly. Fascinated beyond measure, I immediately followed this strange being; and, almost before I was aware of what was happening, found myself racing down the marble steps in close pursuit of it. The peculiarity of its antics increased the further we descended; and at length reached a climax. Suddenly halting on the very margin of a step, it stood on its head and revolved at such a terrific speed that, overcome with dizziness, I fell. I have a vague notion that the figure caught me in its arms as I whizzed past it, and then all was lost in a blinding, deafening, suffocating rush through the air, a rush which terminated not in any conscious transitionary stage, but in my suddenly finding myself in a thickly wooded glade, sitting close beside a waterfall and watching my recent conductor, who was standing on the brink of a deep pool immediately beneath the cascade, bending slowly backwards and forwards, and assuming, every now and then, the most grotesque and extravagant attitude. I was wondering what he meant by these attitudes, when he came to an abrupt pause, and, stooping slightly forward, craned his neck in my direction, and began contorting his face in every conceivable shape, till at last he appeared all mouth. Rushing at me he was about to swallow me, when I awoke.

I had this dream prior to a time when my affairs were singularly prosperous all round, which condition of things was undoubtedly presaged by the lark (a bird of exceptional good omen), by the carnations, pansies, forget-me-nots, and pink and white roses, by the clearness of the water in the river, and by the deep blue of the sea. I cannot attach any meaning to the figure and its strange antics; they form one of those apparently insoluble enigmas that so frequently occur in fantastic phantomnia.

Dream III: A Town

I often dream of the same town. Sometimes all the inhabitants appear wearing costumes of one colour, sometimes all appear wearing costumes of another colour, sometimes they all appear clad in black. Having dreamed one of these dreams quite recently, I append the following description:

I found myself approaching the town from the

direction of a desert. It was a glorious evening, and the walls and windows of the houses shone like burnished gold in the ruddy glow of the slanting sunbeams. But what impressed me on this occasion, over and above all, was the silence; it seemed assumed for a purpose and to be part of a plot, in which everyone and everything participated, and I had the uncomfortable feeling that I was to be the victim of some unpleasant hoax. I cast my eyes in all directions—there was not a soul to be seen—the desert with its interminable extent of brown soil, dotted here and there with spidery looking trees; discovered no one; neither could I discern the slightest evidence of life in the town. Entering a broad, cobble-paved street, I was proceeding slowly along it, almost afraid to tread on account of the clatter made by my boots, when suddenly, without the faintest warning, I was surrounded by a crowd of people, all in brown clothes, and all wearing an air of the greatest mystery. Catching hold of me gently by the arms, with one finger laid on their lips to enjoin silence, they tiptoed cautiously forward, dragging me with them. In this manner we advanced some hundreds of yards, coming to a sudden standstill in front of a kind of brown bathing machine. One of the crowd then stepped forward, and, bowing to me with mock solemnity, very cautiously approached the wooden box. Pausing for a moment to see that everyone was perfectly still, he laid his hand very slowly on the handle of the door, and, amidst the most profound silence, flung it open. Instantly there jumped out on me the most dreadful of creatures, a ghastly caricature of humanity with livid red eyes, and brown face and body, and, as I fled in terror, the houses, walls and people shrieked with laughter. On and on I tore, the sounds of devilish merriment still ringing in my ears, and the ghoulish horror still in hot pursuit. At last, finding that I could hold out no longer, I was about to resign myself to its clutches, when I awoke.

Now, although this dream was decidedly unpleasant, it was the precursor of good fortune. And this I think may be accounted for by the predominance in my dream of brown and gold—the brown in the sand of the desert and dress of the people, the gold in the effects of the sunset.

Dream IV: A CASTLE

I dream I am in the entrance hall of a huge castle. The walls, floor, and ceiling are all of stone. There is no one about, and throughout the vast building reigns an omnipotent hush. Confronting me is a broad spiral staircase, which I proceed to ascend. Up, up, up I go, and I am beginning to despair of ever arriving at the summit, when from far below comes the faint sound of footsteps. I pause to listen, and my blood turns to ice. There is something in those footsteps that suggests the grotesque and sinister. Panic-stricken, I assay to run, and my feet seem weighted with iron. The footsteps grow more and more audible. They are no longer walking but bounding—bounding prodigiously, three stairs at a time. Wild with terror, I struggle feebly on; the footsteps draw nearer and nearer—three stairs—two stairs—one stair—they are on me. I make up my mind I am caught, when behold, they pass me by, and on venturing to look up I see nothing—nothing! and yet the sounds are still going on, up, up, up, until they die away in the interminable heights above me—and all again is wrapt in silence. After a brief pause I continue my ascent, and presently find myself at the entrance to a long stone corridor, pierced with innumerable doorways. There is something so inconceivably grim in the cold, yellow atmosphere of this passage, something so horribly suggestive of a thousand uncanny possibilities in the aspect of its doors, that I stand still, rooted to the ground with terror. Every moment, I expect to see the doors fly open and the horrors they conceal spring out on me. Nothing happening, however, I am congratulating myself that my fears are groundless, when, with an unexpectedness that makes my heart almost leap out of my body, every door opens simultaneously and scores of long, yellow feet appear, which, after striking the ground three times in unison, are hurriedly withdrawn. An interval of some seconds follows, after which the doors are once more opened and the most curious, long, thin, yellow faces, half human and half animal, are thrust through with a mechanical and mirthless "Ha, ha, ha!" These also disappear from view, the doors shutting simultaneously as before. A vast number of footsteps are now heard ascending the staircase, and, almost before I have time to move aside, dozens of tall figures clad in the most fantastic of tight-fitting yellow garments come racing up, and, ranging themselves in two opposite rows right along the corridor, all stamp their feet to the tune of a deep intonated "Hock, hock, hock!" which they repeat in unison. This strange performance goes on for what to me seems an eternity, and just as I am beginning to think it never will terminate, the figures are suddenly quiet, and there appears in their midst a drummer with an enormous, round head, a huge, gaping mouth, and large, round, pale eyes full of an indefinitely peculiar expression; the very vagueness of which is absolutely terrifying. With the same unfathomable expression he flourishes his drumsticks in the air, and as he brings them down with a mighty, hollow-sounding boom, everything changes, and I find myself with hundreds of other people—all apparently equally bereft of reason—racing, as if for dear life, down a vast flight of stone steps. Even as I fly I rack my brains for some explanation of the panic, but, whenever I am on the verge of grasping a solution, it eludes me, and my mind sees nothing but a grey awfulness. Again, and in the twinkling of an eye, the scene changes, and I am in the courtyard of the castle, turning the windlass of a well. Up, up, up comes the bucket, unusually heavy I think for water, and I am about to peer over the edge of the well to see what has happened, when, to my surprise, there rises in sight a huge yellow wheel. Rolling on to the ground it bounds away, and ere I have ceased wondering at its evolutions, a hand touches me lightly on the shoulder, and I find myself face to face with the drummer. The look in his eyes now terrifies me beyond endurance, and I awake.

The yellow in this dream portends treachery; and it is a fact that, shortly after experiencing it, an exceptionally dirty trick was played me by one whom I had hitherto regarded as a friend. The actions and expressions of the dream-people are, at present, enigmatical to me, albeit I cannot help fancying that they are a language in themselves, and that underlying them all, there is much subtle meaning. Wheels and drummers invariably augur ill.

DREAM V: TRAVELLING IN DREAMLAND

Some time ago I dreamed I left my body, and, after travelling at a great rate through the still night air, arrived at the sphere I designate Phantomnia. The spot where I settled down was a lonely railway cutting, and I at once remarked on the loud moaning and sighing of the wind through the telegraph wires, and the curious jar, jar, jar of the iron railroad; and the metals which grew less and less like ordinary metals the longer I looked at them, suddenly became imbued with life, and, rising on end, rushed blindly hither and thither and then lay down again. Presently I heard the whistle of an approaching train. Nearer, nearer, and nearer it came, and as it whizzed past me all the passengers put their heads out of the windows simultaneously, and burst into peal upon peal of mad, hilarious laughter. There was then a tremendous crash, and engine and coaches vanished from sight, over the side of a precipice. The next moment everything changed, and I found myself racing into the railway station to get my ticket. The place was absolutely deserted, not a porter nor a passenger anywhere, and the train all ready to go. The office was shut, as is always the case when we are in a desperate hurry in Phantomnia; but, being determined to make the clerk hear, I commenced a vigorous cannonade with my fist on the pigeon-hole door. Presently the latter flew open, and out popped a bald, white head, with such evil, lurid eyes and sinister smile that, shocked beyond measure, I staggered back. As I did so, I came into collision with a porter, who, without asking my permission, unceremoniously shoved me into a train, and, before I could recover my breath, we were off. The compartment, in which I found myself, was at least three times the size of any I had hitherto seen. It was already full of white-faced people, who, sitting and lying among innumerable boxes in, apparently, the most uncomfortable postures, were fast asleep and snoring—snoring to the most fantastic and taking of tunes I have ever heard. My not having a ticket greatly perturbed me. I expected every moment the collector would put in an appearance and make a scene, and, sure enough, in accordance with my forebodings, in he came, accompanied by the guard, engine-driver; foreman, and half-a-dozen other officials, who; rushing on me with livid faces and flashing eyes; were about to annihilate me altogether when a tremendous hubbub on the line attracted the attention of one and all, and a most extraordinary spectacle presented itself to our gaze. Exactly opposite our compartment was a monstrous green engine that was alternately jumping up and down, and rearing up, first on one end and then on the other, after the manner of a shying horse. The jumps eventually getting higher and higher, the engine at last jumped so high that it jumped out of sight, whereupon passengers and officials, with agonised shrieks and wails, climbed out of the doors and windows of the train; and, rushing across the fields, plunged en masse into a muddy, roaring river. I now found myself the only passenger in a train that, without either engine or officials, was stranded in one of the wildest and weirdest spots imagination could conceive. Ghastly as was the appearance of the muddy, turbulent river, that of the hedges separating the railroad from the fields was even more so, for although at first sight they seemed ordinary enough, on closer inspection they proved to be no hedges at all, but long rows of grotesque creatures, black and green—half human and half bestial—that, clutching hold of and encircling each other's waists with their arms, swayed to and fro with ill-suppressed laughter. As I stared at them they suddenly shook themselves free, and with heads lowered so that I could perceive nothing of their faces, came bounding toward me over the grass.

By a merciful providence, the train now took it into its head to move, and, getting up a tremendous speed, it was soon travelling along at a record pace; indeed, it went so fast that the coaches eventually left the rails, and it was their continual bump, bump, bump on hilltops and trees that awoke me.

The significant features of the dream may be characterised thus: Travelling per train portended trouble; the accident I witnessed, danger from drowning, which was further emphasised by the muddiness of the river; the extreme pallor of the passengers' faces indicating death. The dream was shortly afterwards verified by the drowning of an old and valued friend in one of the American rivers; and by my own personal worries which were at that time considerable, both with regard to financial affairs and also in connection with my work.

Dream VI: A Storm

I have, over and over again in my dreams, visited a certain district when the weather has been fine; but the other night I was there during a storm, and the experience, though interesting, was not too agreeable. I was in a hut on a wide, vast desert traversed by a broad river, and bounded by a long chain of mountains on the one side, and on the other by a forest of pines. On my arrival all was hushed and still; the air soft and sweet; the sky clear and blue; typical in every respect of an ideal summer day. The change was brought about in a totally unprecedented manner. The blue of the heavens was suddenly metamorphosed into a vivid violet, and the wind from the mountain tops, shrieking and roaring like ten million devils across the plain, converted the hitherto placid waters of the rivers into raging rapids; and then, tearing past my hut with the thunder of hell, hurled every tree in the forest to the ground. The effect of the sky was now apparent in everything; the whole landscape—mountains, river, and sands, and even the prostrate forest—shone with a violet glow. So far the rain had held off, but presently a huge hand was thrust out of the sky and shaken menacingly, whereupon a great fissure opened, and a whole sea of bubbling, violet water descended with such terrific force that the earth gave way beneath it; and amidst an inferno of sand, rafters, and water I was borne down, down, till all became suffused in the blackness of hell—and I lost consciousness. On recovery, I was standing knee-deep in an ocean of violet water that seethed and hissed on all sides of me. From time to time the dull glow around me was transformed into a lurid sheet of violet fire by the lightning, whilst the sky heaved up and down in the most terrifying manner as it volleyed forth peal after peal of demoniacal thunder. And amidst all this titanic uproar a long slender hand arose out of the water, and, turning slowly round, clenched and unclenched its white, tapering fingers three times, and then sank out of sight. Instantly the wind, and the thunder, and the hissing and seething of the waters ceased; the lake at my feet disappeared; the trees and hut sprang up; the sky shone and all was once again as before the storm. And thus the dream ended.

In this dream, which ended happily, the violet signified success appertaining to the arts; and the storm, followed by a general reparation of all the mischief it had done, portended a quarrel, which, although serious at the time, would have no lasting result. It was soon verified in the case of a very near and dear friend of mine. Success in a special branch of his work led to a violent quarrel, and this quarrel, contrary to both his and my expectations, being eventually bridged over, the former friendship was re-established, and, so far, has continued without another interruption.

Dream VII: DREAMLAND HUNTSMEN

Huntsmen not infrequently figure in my dreams. On July 1st, 1909, I dreamed I was standing on the verandah of a house, overlooking a neatly kept lawn and a broad white carriage drive, beyond which was a spinney. It was a beautiful evening, and every object stood out with startling perspicuity in the powerful moonlight. Whilst I was gazing admiringly at the transcendental loveliness of the landscape, I felt a soft hand laid caressingly on my arm, and, on looking round, saw a lady clad in the costume of the middle ages. As she often figures in my dreams, I was in no degree astonished at her appearance. "How romantic we are!" she said, with a smile; "I was quite under the impression that lingering so long in a great city had spoilt you for the pleasures of the country. With me it is too much country, I long for the town—for the theatre! Cannot we go there to-night?" "To-night!" I ejaculated; "say rather to-morrow!" "No! to-night," she answered, with a pout of her pretty lips; "you always try to disappoint me but I WILL have my way this time, you shall see! I will summon the horses!" She clapped her tiny, bejewelled hands together as she spoke. There was a loud clatter of hoofs, and the next instant two silver-grey, fiery-eyed horses trotted in at the front gates and galloped across the lawn. "Come!" she cried, seizing me by the arm, "let us be off at once!" Yielding to her wishes, I followed her out of the house and on to the lawn; where the steeds stood impatiently pawing the ground. Leaping nimbly on to one of them, she looked down at me with an artful smile on her bewitching lips, and crying out: "Through the wood! Through the wood! Beware of the huntsman in the green hood!" struck the animal across the neck with her whip and was off like an arrow, whilst the sound of her words "Through the wood! through the wood!" etc., echoed and re-echoed through the still night air till every stone, and stick, and blade of grass seemed to take it and bellow it in my ears. It was in vain I tried to mount and follow. Every time I tried to get my foot in the stirrup, the beast slipped away from me, and I narrowly escaped a tumble. At last, in desperation, I made a frantic rush, but my steed melted into nothingness, and the next moment I found myself racing through the spinney in hot pursuit of my wayward companion. On and on I tore but no sign of the horse and its rider, only the shadows from the great, gaunt trees that stole out one by one to look at me. At length I came to an opening in the wood, in the centre of which was a fountain; and standing by it, with his back to me, I saw the figure of a man in a tight-fitting suit of Lincoln green, his head covered with a hood, a quiver full of arrows at his side, and a bow in his right hand. At the sight of him my heart leaped into my mouth, for I guessed, at once, he was the huntsman of whom I had so emphatically been told to beware. Had I not been prevented by one of those spells so common in dreams, I should have turned back, but try how I would I could not stir from the spot, and I had no choice other than to stand there, sick with suspense and trepidation. Though I had not as yet seen it, the face of the huntsman was what I feared most. It is the faces—always the faces—of these grotesque-looking individuals in my dreamland that are so alarming. As minute after minute passed and still he did not turn round, my anticipation at length grew to such a pitch that, unable to restrain myself any longer, I shrieked to heaven for pity; upon which he swung round and his countenance was fully revealed. So strong were the moonbeams —far stronger than they are in actuality—that every feature in his face stood out as clearly as if I had seen them through a magnifying-glass. The nose was hawk-like, prominent and curved, the chin—long and pointed, the eyebrows—black and slanting; and the eyes—God help me!—only a lurid, satanic glitter proceeding from the innermost recesses of the skull. The face was fleshless and the skin, which was white and luminous, hung closely to the bones, which in places had broken completely through it. It was the face of the long since dead animated by the spirit of a devil, and I doubt if even the Hell of Dante could show such another. Familiar as I was with the sight of ghastly phantasms of all kinds, I had never seen one that impressed me with quite such a terror as this, and, as it glided slowly towards me with outstretched arms, I verily believe my heart would have burst asunder and I should have died in my sleep, had not the spell that held me limb-tied been suddenly broken. With wild shrieks of despair I fled away, and from behind every bush and tree darted, similarly apparelled, huntsmen in close pursuit. Every now and then, there was a loud twang and an arrow whizzed past my ears, whilst all my pursuers joined in shouting at the top of their harsh, shrill voices, "Through the wood; through the wood! Beware of the huntsman in the green hood." With their shouts ringing louder and louder in my ears, I was fast coming to an end of my tether, when there was a blinding flash of jagged, blood-red lightning, and I found myself in the market square of a mediæval town. The place was full of people, all wearing green costumes of the fashion of the fifteenth century, and on my appearance, they all began to dance. Not a word was spoken by anyone, and not a sound was heard beyond the incessant tapping of feet on the cobblestones, which continued until, as if in obedience to some unheard command, everyone was suddenly motionless. There was then a great stir and the crowd, moving away, bore me with them through innumerable streets—streets that, narrow and winding, and crossing each other irregularly in all directions, were in reality alleys. The houses in them were fantastically picturesque. At all the windows stood, or leaned, men, and women, and queer looking things for which I can find no suitable name—they were part human and part animal—and all shouted, and yelled, and gesticulated, regardless of sense and order. At last, when the confusion had reached a climax, the crowd, again obeying some secret order, dived up another street, and the most deathlike hush ensued. Then, from far away in the distance, came the pattering of many soft-clad feet, and a long procession filed past me —knights in armour on richly caparisoned horses, standard bearers, palanquins, litters with fair-haired ladies, men-at-arms, archers, drums, trumpets, spears, silver and gilded maces, troupe after troupe of merry-eyed dancing girls, followed by a hundred or so of the same queer-looking creatures I saw at the windows, carrying triangles in one hand and scales in the other; and last—last of all—mounted on a gigantic white horse, the tall and gaunt figure of Death. He wore nothing save two long, green feathers which waved to and fro, in the most ludicrous fashion, as he bowed his fleshless head, first on one side and then on the other, in gracious acknowledgment of the salutes of the people. And what a reception he had! A reception in which everyone joined, young and old, rich and poor, from those on the housetops, and balconies, and in doorways, and windows, even to those in the procession itself! One and all shouted and cheered, clapped, stamped, and yelled with glee; and then—then without the slightest warning the air resounded with shrieks of terror, and, on straining my neck to perceive the cause, I saw advancing up the street towards where I stood dozens of greenclad huntsmen, who were discharging their arrows indiscriminately at the revellers. In less time than it takes to tell the crowd vanished, and I found myself flying through street after street, now all silent and deserted, pursued by the huntsmen, whose hoarse cries curdled my blood. At last I came to a vast, white building, and across it was written in blood-red letters, "The Fountain Theatre." Without stopping to ask permission; into it I dashed. A play was going on, and as I entered everyone including the performers, shook their fists at me and hooted. Then, like magic, the place emptied and I found myself—the only audience present—sitting in the front row of the stalls, gazing at the stage, which, like the entire auditorium, was bathed in funereal gloom. Presently a hollow sounding clock boomed twelve, and, ere the last notes had died away, the orchestra filled with vast formless things that, seating themselves, evidently in their accustomed places, at the signal of their conductor beat their spectral palms frantically together. On to the stage from either wing there then wriggled and writhed in ghastly imitation of worms, shapes which suggested more than I dare to name—and which I shrank from analysing. And whilst they were in the midst of their hateful evolutions, a cloud of arrows suddenly burst upon them, and, on looking round, I saw, to my terror, that boxes, circles, and gallery were filled with huntsmen, who now levelled their bows at me. A thousand burning pains rushed through my body, and as the agony of my soul found vent in one loud and final scream of horror and despair, I rose to my feet, staggered forward, tottered, and, amidst the discordant hum of harsh, inhuman voices—woke.

The significant features of this dream; which I am now able to interpret, are as follows: The white steeds signify preservation from danger; the green in the costumes of the huntsmen, and in the plumes of Death, signify the advent of some psychic experience; the figure of Death points to a birth, engagement, or marriage; the triangles are symbolic of the counteracting of evil by good influences; the dancing, of impending minor disappointments; the mimicry of worms, of recovery from illness, and success in histrionism.

My dream was fulfilled within a week in the following manner: I narrowly escaped a serious accident; I heard of the engagement of the sister of my greatest friend to a man of exceptionally fine character; I encountered evil influences, which I succeeded in dispelling, in a haunted house; I was unable to accept an offer from a firm, with whom I had particularly wished to publish, owing to lack of time; and I took part, unexpectedly, in a theatrical performance that was voted a great success.

DREAM VIII: DREAMLAND ANIMALS

One night, as far back as 1894, I dreamed I was in a desert in Phantomnia, and that bounding towards me from a distance, came a white kangaroo decorated with large, brown spots that looked as if they had been recently painted, and which imparted to it a wooden appearance. It came right up to me, and eyeing me in the most friendly manner possible, said, "Have you seen my mother?" "No!" I replied, "I have not seen anyone here for the last two years, because it is fully that time since I visited these parts. What is she like?" The kangaroo was greatly perplexed. "Why," he said; "to tell you the truth I haven't the slightest idea. I thought, perhaps, you might know; but, of course; since you have been absent for so long, it is very obvious you are the last person I should have asked. Good-bye." And, with a leap, he was gone. I shouted out to him, "Why not ask that tree?" (there was a poplar growing near) but he did not hear me, and was out of sight before I could speak again.

I walked on, but had not gone very far, before I came across a boy standing on a big stone, and blowing out his cheeks. There was a look of the most exquisite joy in his round, gooseberry eyes, as if he found his occupation the most delightful in the world. "Why, what on earth are you doing?" I asked. He opened his mouth and out flew a swarm of bees. "Oh! isn't it Paradise?" he said. "Paradise! they make their honey in my stomach!" "But don't they sting you?" I asked. "Well, now you come to speak of it, I believe they do," the boy responded, "but what is that compared with the honey! Besides, see the amount of labour it saves!" and with that he started whistling. I cannot recollect the air, but it must have been something very infectious, for much as I hate dancing I took off my coat, and holding it straight in front of me commenced to waltz. "And why not your trousers, too?" whistled the boy, "you don't want them. You are only a monkey." I looked down, and the first thing I saw was my tail, that sat up on end and laughed at me. "Well, really, things have come to a fine point!" I exclaimed, "the lower orders making fun of the upper in this fashion! What next shall we hear!" "You can't do two things at once," sneered the tail, "you can't dance and scold me.

Either you must go on dancing and leave me behind or—or——" and, suddenly becoming greatly confused, it whirled round and round at a tremendous rate until it tied itself up in a hopeless knot. "If that isn't a misfortune, I don't know what it is!" whistled the boy. "Have some honey?"

"But how am I to get it?" I enquired. "I can't cut you open!"

"If you were not quite so big," he said, "I should suggest you let yourself down into my inside by your tail, but alas! it's your size that's in the way. And, after all, honey may not be good for you!"

"That is because you want it all for yourself," I cried, trying in vain to stop dancing, and all but tripping over my partner, who had the most irritating knack of flapping between my legs.

"Life is full of gluttons," whistled the boy. "I'm one, you're one, and so is your partner," and, leaving off whistling, he turned very pale and pointed excitedly at my coat. Following his glance, the blood in my veins froze. My coat, which was buttoned, had swollen to an enormous size, and right across the back of it, was a huge, flabby-lipped mouth that was gulping down some nasty-looking, sticky mess as fast as it could. With an ejaculation of disgust I loosened my hold of it, and the next moment, caught up by a strong current of air, it was wafted away from me and borne at a great rate across the desert. Hanging on to it behind, I noticed (with the greatest sensation of relief) my tail! I now left the boy, and aiming for a clump of trees I saw in the distance, was rapidly advancing towards it, when a very tall and thin man, with a flat rectangular face no thicker than a plank, rose out of a pit a few yards away from me, and in a quavering falsetto voice cried out to me to stop. Complying with his request, I approached the edge of the pit, when out of it sprang an enormous lion. It had hurled me to the ground, and was in the act of mauling my throat, when I awoke.

I interpret the foregoing dream thus:

The kangaroo signified a journey; the bees, success in financial matters; dancing, minor troubles; whistling, a lover's quarrel; the metamorphose to a monkey, the breaking off of a marriage through my agency; the lion, marriage.

Shortly after this dream I went to the Pacific Coast of America; a great friend of mine was very successful in his speculations on the Stock Exchange but was much worried over a series of troubles at home; whilst another friend, equally dear to me, foolishly got engaged to the daughter of a nouveau riche who was vulgar even for a parvenu.

A quarrel arising between them, owing to her grossly snobbish behaviour to some of his poor, albeit presentable, relations, he came to me for advice, and although I make a strong point of never interfering where love is concerned, I considered this an exceptional case, and strongly urged him to break off the engagement. He acted on my counsel, and within six weeks the girl married someone in her own set, as vulgar and pretentious as herself.

CHAPTER VI

REPETITIONARY AND PECULIARLY VIVID DREAMS

I BELIEVE there are people who dream the same dreams repeatedly, even down to the most minute details. One of the dreams I am continually dreaming is as follows: I am walking along the sea-front of some popular watering-place, which, judging by the style of houses and appearance of the people, I should say was abroad. The sun is shining, the sea exquisitely blue; whilst, to enhance the beauty of nature, a band is playing, and playing remarkably well, some gay operatic music. What I see, what I feel, what I think, has about it nothing of the unmistakeable idiosyncrasy of a dream, but all is rigorously self-consistent. I am enjoying myself to the utmost, when, on turning round, I perceive behind me a tramp—a man with a shock head of red hair, and features that are ineffaceably stamped on my memory. He is a blight, a sore, a gangrene in this place of beauty, cleanliness and elegance; and as I am wondering at the strange incongruity of it, he solicits me for alms. I refuse.

He asks again. I threaten him with the police. He is at once silent. Turning my back on him, I continue my promenade. Some one in the street utters a cry of horror. I swing round, and as I do so, the tramp stabs me in the back. I catch a look of hellish vindictiveness in his ferretty eyes, and then, seized with an instantaneous and dreadful sickness, I stagger, reel and fall, struggle, gasp—and die!

I think this dream must be intended as a warning, and I never visit a fresh seaside place—particularly abroad—without considerable anxiety as to the appearance of the front. So far, I have found no place to correspond quite with that in my dream.

In other dreams I continually visit the same places, sometimes—a waterfall, sometimes—a river flowing through a dense wood, sometimes—a farm-house; and on each occasion the incidents are strictly repetitionary. Close beside the waterfall I fish, and am always in the act of landing a huge trout, when my tackle gets entangled in some hyper-extraordinary fashion, and I awake. I wander along a shady road by the side of the river, and always at a certain opening an old man, staggering beneath a load of sticks, crosses my path and enters the wicket-gate leading to a tiny, white-washed and neatly thatched cottage. The man has a black patch over one eye, very thick white hair, and is clean-shaven. He wears a white jacket with bone buttons, corduroy trousers, and shoes, one of which is fastened with common or garden string. I have certainly never visited such a spot nor seen such a person, except in my dreams, and can only conclude that it must either be a forecast of what is to happen to me some day, or that projection takes place during sleep and I visit the actual spot in my immaterial body. This unconscious projection, as may be proved by many authentic cases, is by no means an uncommon occurrence, and I am of the opinion that many vivid scenic dreams may thus be explained. One of the best-known stories, illustrating the theory of projection during sleep, is to this effect. A Miss G——, who dreamed so frequently of an old country house that she got to know every nook and cranny of it by heart, went on a visit to some friends with whom she had never stayed before. The moment she caught sight of their house she recognised it ; and her identification was startlingly corroborated by the servants, who, unable to restrain their excitement on seeing her, simultaneously exclaimed, "The ghost ! The ghost !" It then transpired that, for some time past, the house had been haunted by the phantasm of a lady corresponding in every detail to Miss

G——; and as Miss G—— was found to be as familiar with every room and passage of the house as if she had lived there all her life, it could only be deducted that she had constantly visited the place in her immaterial body, and that it was her immaterial body (projection) that had been seen by various inmates of the house and taken for a ghost.

T. Charley, in his *News from the Invisible World*, quotes the following curious example of a murder prevented by a thrice-fold dream:

"Monday, April 2, 1781, I was informed by a person in an eminent station of a very uncommon incident. He had occasion to correct with a few stripes a lad that lived with him at Rochester; and the lad, resenting the punishment, left. But some time after, on the youth appearing to repent of his behaviour and humbling himself accordingly, he was received into the house again, when he behaved in a most becoming manner and was doubly diligent in his service.

"One night his mistress dreamed that this lad was going to cut her throat; and, as if the dream was not of sufficient significance in itself, she shortly afterwards had a letter from a sister stating that she, too, had dreamed the very same thing. The lady at once took the letter to her father, who lived not very far off, and was surprised to hear that he, likewise, on the same night, had a dream to the same effect. The youth was then closely watched, and on being observed to come up, about noon one day, to the door of his mistress's apartment with a case-knife in his hand, he was stopped, and an explanation of his conduct was demanded. In reply, he said he intended going into the adjoining room—*i.e.*, the room leading out of his mistress's—to scrape the dirt off his master's embroidered shirt.

"The answer not being deemed at all satisfactory, he was taken aside and put to a searching examination, when he ended by confessing "that he had always remembered with indignation his master's severity to him, and had fully resolved on revenge," but in what manner he would not say. He was, of course, instantly discharged; and the lady and her husband congratulated themselves on their escape from a horrible death—an escape which they confessed was entirely owing to the dreams."

DREAMS OF CONTEMPORARY EVENTS

There are unquestionably certain people who, in their dreams, witness events that are actually taking place at the time.

A lady I knew, Mrs. P——, who lived in Gloucester Place, W., dreamed one night she was in a big seaport town, where the streets were all numbered and laid out in blocks according to the American system, and where in one part of the city the tram-lines descended over a series of plateaux. The houses were very lofty, and in one street a single hotel occupied an entire block. Shortly after her arrival, the entire town shook and heaved under the influence of a stupendous earthquake; houses collapsed like packs of cards, and, amidst the most appalling shrieks and groans, the whole city burst into a lurid sheet of fire. Everywhere was the wildest confusion and despair. People of all nationalities, from fair-skinned Europeans and yellow-visaged Chinese—of which there were legions— to swarthy Dagos and bullet-headed negroes, vied with one another in their mad efforts to escape the falling bricks and burning timber. In trying to elude one death men only courted another, and the dreamer saw scores of human beings who leaped from burning buildings, only to be dashed to pieces on the cruel stone pavements. Nor was the heroic element wanting, for many men and women perished in their efforts to rescue the infirm and sick, and to help those to escape, who were either too old or too young to help themselves. For some time, the dreamer was merely a spectator, but very suddenly, and by some inconceivable impulse, she became imbued with personal interest in what was going on, and, labouring under the impression that her home and family were in danger, fought her way to get to them. The city was now no longer strange to her, and she found herself turning first to the right and then to the left in the most familiar and natural manner possible, until she came to 119th Street, where her anxious eyes immediately travelled to the house she imagined was her own. It was a mass of flames, and at one of the windows she saw the white and agonised faces of her husband and children.

With the fury of a tigress she beat and pushed her way through the dense crowd of fugitives, whom she besought—but besought in vain—to assist her in the rescue of her family. Eventually she arrived opposite her house. Her husband and youngest child were still at the window clawing frantically at the iron bars, through which neither of them could crawl, and as soon as they saw her they yelled and grinned, and thrust out their hands at her. As she gazed at them, dumb with the agony of despair, there was a hideous rending, tearing and tottering of woodwork and masonry, the entire building fell to the ground with the noise of thunder, and, with this appalling crash still resonating in her ears, Mrs. P—— awoke. This dream occurred contemporary with the last great fire and earthquake at San Francisco, and those to whom she narrated it—namely, those who, like myself, knew the city—were assured that her description of it was exact in every detail. Here again projection may explain much.

Mrs. P——, forewarned by a superphysical power of a danger threatening those between whom and herself there was a strong bond of spiritual sympathy, had in her sleep unconsciously projected herself to the spot where the catastrophe was taking place, hoping thereby to save those she loved from their impending fate.

T. Charley, in his *News from the Invisible World*, furnishes another example of this type of dream, namely, as follows:

"Dr. Donne and his wife lived for some time in London with Sir Robert Daury. Sir Robert having occasion to go to Paris, took the doctor along with him, leaving his wife, who was in a delicate state of health, at Sir Robert's house. Two days after their arrival at Paris, Dr. Donne was left alone in the room where Sir Robert, and he, and some other friends had dined together. Sir Robert returned in half an hour, and as he had left so he found the doctor, alone; but in such an ecstasy and so altered in his looks as amazed Sir Robert to behold. He inquired the cause, and after some time the doctor told him he had seen a dreadful vision. 'I beheld,' he said, 'my dear wife pass twice by me through this room, with her hair hanging about her shoulders and a dead child in her arms.' A messenger was immediately despatched to England to inquire after Mrs. Donne; and it appeared that, at the very time Dr. Donne affirmed he had seen her, their child had died, and she had been completely prostrated with grief."

In this case I am inclined to believe the vision was due to projection on the part of Mrs. Donne—which projection had taken place during the delirium characteristic of her illness—and that the figures seen by Dr. Donne were actually those of her astral body and the spirit of the dead child.

Of course, I do not assert that all vivid dreams are due to projection; many, I know, are merely caused by an over-tired or excited brain going through a recapitulation of the events of the day. For instance, when I was about fourteen years of age and at a public school, I was put under gas during the extraction of a couple of very firmly rooted grinders. Owing to some difficulty the dentist had in extracting them, I "came to" before the operation was over, and suffered agonies. That night in my sleep I again went through the grim proceedings, detail for detail, from my entry into the surgery and the anxious gaze around for the dreaded instruments, to the final look at the gold-fish in the aquarium, before my jaws were propped open, and my nose and mouth enveloped in the soft and spongy cap, I had so uneasily remarked in the hands of the anæsthetist. Again I smelt the sweet and sickly odour of the gas; again I heard the voices of the doctor and dentist growing fainter and fainter till they died away altogether; and again there was a sudden blank, followed by an excruciating pain, in which I seemed to feel the entire upper part of my head slowly wrenched away from the lower. Youth undoubtedly magnifies all things—joys and sorrows and pains; and in our after-life we do not feel things so acutely as we did in our childhood. The torture of the rack, I am sure, was as nothing compared with the torture I endured in my sleep under those forceps; and then—blessed relief!—the diabolical cause of my suffering flew out, and the vague unearthly hum of voices grew louder and louder, till they finally became recognisable human accents; when, as I had actually done under the anæsthetic, I awoke. But it was all real—cruelly, wickedly real; and it was due, I have no doubt, to the over-tired condition of my brain, which allowed the hyper-morbid memory-cells to have it all their own way.

DREAMS OF THE DEAD

It is by no means uncommon to dream of the dead, and as a rule such dreams are of little or no significance. There are, however, exceptions, as, for example, dreams which are extraordinarily vivid and in which the dead appear with some specific purpose; and in these cases I fancy projections take place, and the immaterial body of the sleeper meets the phantasm of the dead on the superphysical plane.

For the following illustration of this kind of dream I am again indebted to *News from the Invisible World.* The events in the story, I am about to quote, happened about seventy years ago in the south of Scotland.

"Mr. Reid, of Bowland, a gentleman of landed property in the Vale of Gala, was prosecuted for a very considerable sum, the accumulated arrears of tithes, for which he was said to be indebted to a noble family, the lay proprietors.

"Mr. Reid was strangely impressed with the belief that his father had (by a form of process peculiar to the law of Scotland) purchased these lands from the titular, and, therefore, that the present prosecution was groundless. But after an investigation of the public records, and a careful inquiry among all persons who had transacted law business for his father, no evidence could be recovered to support his defence. The period was now near at hand when he conceived the loss of his lawsuit inevitable, and he had formed his determination to ride to Edinburgh next day, and make the best bargain he could in the way of compromise. He went to bed with this resolution, and, with all the circumstances of the case floating upon his mind, had a dream to the following purpose.

"His father, who had been many years dead, appeared to him, he thought, and asked him why he was disturbed in his mind. In dreams men are not surprised at such apparitions. Mr. Reid thought that he informed his father of the cause of his distress, adding that the payment of a considerable sum of money was the more unpleasant to him, because he had a strong consciousness that it was not due, though he was unable to recover any evidence in support of his belief. 'You are right, my son,' replied the paternal shade, 'I did acquire rights to these tithes, for payment of which you are now prosecuted. The papers relating to the transactions are in the hands of Mr. ——, an attorney, who is now retired from professional business and resides at Inveresk, near Edinburgh. He was the person whom I employed on that occasion for a particular reason; but who never on any other occasion transacted business on my account. It is very possible,' pursued the vision, 'that Mr. —— may have forgotten a circumstance which is now of very old date; but you may call it to his recollection by this token, that when I came to pay him his account there was difficulty in getting change for a Portugal piece of gold, and that we were forced to drink out the balance at a tavern.'

"Mr. Reid awaked in the morning with all the words of the vision imprinted on his mind, and resolved to ride across the country to Inveresk, instead of going straight to Edinburgh. When he came there he waited on the gentleman mentioned in the dream. Without saying anything of the vision, he inquired whether he remembered having conducted such a matter for his father. The old gentleman could not at first bring the circumstances to his recollection, but on the mention of the Portugal piece of gold the whole returned upon his memory. He made an immediate search for the papers, and recovered them; so that Mr. Reid was thus, by the instrumentality of his vision, enabled to carry to Edinburgh the documents necessary to gain the cause, which he was on the verge of losing." Here the account ends.

I think a feasible explanation of the dream is, that it was in reality a case of unconscious projection during sleep, when the spirit of Mr. Reid was disembodied through the agency of his dead father, who, having something of such vital importance to communicate, was thus permitted to converse with the phantasm of his son on the superphysical plane.

Lady B——, with whom I am slightly acquainted, once had a very vivid dream of this description.

She had been left a widow for some time, and was contemplating marrying again, when she dreamed one night she met her late husband on the margin of a beautiful lake. She went up to him and, laying her hand on his arm, said, "I know you will not object to anything that will promote my happiness. I am thinking of marrying!" Regarding her with a look of the greatest kindness and affection, the phantasm remained silent for a few minutes, and then replied, "No, I object to nothing that will ensure your happiness; but marriage with Mr. S—— will have an opposite result. He does not love you, he only wants your money. If you wish to know more—to find out what manner of man he really is, write to Mr. Scott-Tanner, of West Watling Street, Brisbane, enclosing your fiancé's photograph." The phantasm then kissed her, and, with the impression of his lips still upon hers, she awoke. Much startled by the dream, Lady B—— carried out the instructions contained in it ; and in due course of time actually received a reply, stating that, from the photo and the description she gave of Mr. S——, there could be little doubt that he was a scoundrel of the name of Grigson, who, a few days after his marriage with Scott-Tanner's daughter, had absconded, taking with him all her jewellery and other valuables. Lady B—— now felt constrained to put the matter in the hands of a detective ; but before she had time to carry out her resolution, her would-be bridegroom disappeared, and nothing more was heard of him.

Here again I am inclined to attribute the dream to projection ; and in this case I think the projection of Lady B—— was brought about through the friendly connivance of her dead husband, who, eager to save her from an awful fate, was for that reason permitted to converse with her on the superphysical plane.

RELIGIOUS DREAMS

Instances in which people owe their "conversions" to dreams are not confined to the Scriptures, but are as common to-day as at any other period of the world's history.

I have frequently questioned men as to the causes that led to their "conversion," and have occasionally elicited very curious replies. A Salvationist, for example, related the following dream, assuring me that he owed his conversion entirely to it. "I was a terrible drunkard," he said, "I drained oceans—beer, gin, brandy, methylated spirits were all the same to me; and I more often fell asleep in a dustbin than in a bed. Well, one night I dreamed I was a chimney-pot amid a veritable sea of chimney-pots of all sorts and descriptions. At first, the air, blowing up through me, was cool and pleasant, but it gradually grew hotter and hotter, and more and more smoky, until I suffered the tortures of the damned. My sides blistered, burned and cracked, and I gasped, panted and choked. 'You are on fire!' a cowl close beside me shrieked out, 'on fire! Eugh! How disgusting! We shall all get black and sooty!'

"'Yes, listen to him roaring!' shouted another,

'and see how the red sparks fly! I hope he will speedily break, and then there will be an end to him!' 'That can never be!' thundered the voice of a gigantic, bronze weather-cock in mid-air. 'He is doomed to suffer to eternity; the fire that burns within him is inextinguishable!'

"'Who is that speaking?' a meek little chimney-pot whispered.

"'What, don't you know?' snapped a very tall and angular cowl. 'That is Moses—Moses, the usurper of Heaven—Moses the Jew! He is now visiting every city in the world in the guise of a weathercock. . . . I felt all along that chimney-pot was very wicked,' he said, addressing Moses. 'What are his sins?'

"'He is a drunkard!' the weathercock ejaculated sternly. 'A drunkard! He drinks every drop of rain that falls on the tiles!'

"'The beast!' all the cowls and chimney-pots shouted. 'The beast! Let us hope that he is suffering.'

"'Have no fear on that account,' Moses replied; 'he is connected with the kitchen range, and I have given the chef strict orders to cook a forty-course dinner every night!'

"'And can't I have even one drop of gravy?' I groaned.

"'Not a drop,' growled the weathercock, 'for the dinners are *damned*, and so are you!'—which so frightened me," added the Salvationist, "that I awoke, and from that very day to this have never tasted a thimbleful of alcohol."

Another Salvationist, who attracted my attention by the vigorous manner in which he pounded the drum, informed me he owed the fact of his now being saved—and he seemed to regard it as a very sure fact—to a dream that occurred to him when he had sunk as low as any man could sink.

"I had squandered two entire fortunes in drink," he said, "and, from living in a house of my own in Cadogan Gardens, was reduced to a garret in the South Lambeth Road. Not being brought up to any profession or trade, and having a serious physical defect, I could obtain no regular employment, but had to look out for odd jobs, such, for example, as carrying bags, opening carriage doors, and cleaning the brasswork and windows of public-houses; and all the money I received I spent in drink. My wife had very rightly and wisely obtained a divorce from me. I was dead to all sense of decency and shame, and God alone knows in what act of outrageous devilry my wickedness might not have culminated, had it not been for the arrestive nature of the dream He sent me. I dreamed

I was playing cards in a large, brilliantly illuminated nursery, my adversary being a child of about six years of age, who was seated directly opposite me. In his face and features I had little difficulty in recognising myself—that is to say, myself of long ago, when I was young and pure, without any knowledge save of what was innocent. We played some curious game that was quite new to me and which, strive how I would, I have never been able to recollect since. It was a game of speculation, and the stakes ran high, my opponent winning everything—everything, till at length I had nothing left to risk but my soul, which I staked and lost. I was then so maddened that I sprang from my seat and, seizing a knife, rushed on him and, despite the earnestness with which he pleaded, flung him on the floor, and would have stabbed him, had not the room suddenly become pitch dark, and a loud and hollow voice uttered these words : 'Fool! *Thou hast murdered thine own soul! Know thy hell!*' Something then struck me heavily on the forehead, I lost consciousness, and on recovering, found myself in a huge kitchen garden. A spade was in my hand, and I was digging for potatoes. The sun was so tremendously hot ; my back and arms ached cruelly ; and I was desperately thirsty. 'Curse it!' I said to myself. 'I have had enough of it! The old lady may go without her dinner for all I care! I am not going to wear my self to pieces and get sunstroke for her!' Then I dashed my spade to the ground, and, looking round, espied a pool of clear water. Revelling in the prospect of being now able to quench my thirst, I hastened to the pool, and, kneeling down, dipped my mouth in it. But alas! try how I would, I couldn't drink the water—every time I touched it with my lips it slipped away and I gulped at nothing. With a tin dipper, that I found lying close beside me, I tried to ladle the water out of the pool, but all to no purpose—the water was in the pool, and in the pool it meant to stay. At last, worn out with trying to coax the water into my mouth, and perceiving some luscious-looking plums growing on a tree near by, I resolved to slake my thirst with them instead. But the moment I touched a plum it changed into a reel of cotton. One plum after another I touched, but there was no exception to the rule; and when at last I beheld the plum-tree, upon which I had built such hopes, groaning beneath the weight of countless reels of cotton,I gave way to an outburst of demoniacal fury. Seizing my spade, I struck at the tree again and again, till I had lopped off all the branches and the pond was covered knee-deep in debris. I then essayed to get back to the potato plot, but found I could not stir—I had walled myself in, and the cotton had twisted itself in countless layers round my legs, binding them firmly together. In this deplorable plight I was compelled to stand hour after hour with the sun scorching me mercilessly, and my throat becoming more and more parched and blocked. I cannot describe the sufferings I endured; no devil in hell could have fared worse. At length I fainted; there was a delicious blank, and on coming to myself the garden had vanished, and I found that I was—well, it took me a long time to make out what I was, but I at length discovered—that I was a pair of high-heeled boots, and that I had on the top of me a pair of feet—red-hot, perspiring feet that chafed my skin, squashed me in all my most tender parts, and dragged me with them over sharp, jagged stones, hot asphalt pavements—the smell of which made me retch and vomit—dusty roads that blinded me, and tarry roads that stuck together my lips and eyelids. The torments of purgatory are not to be compared with those I was now compelled to undergo. Whenever I endeavoured to halt, the toe-nails stabbed me in the stomach, the ankle bones prodded my ribs, and the heels came down with extra pressure on my liver—a combination of tortures no one could endure. On and on I toiled, and one and all mocked me.

"'He! he! he!' laughed the garbage in the gutter, 'you've got a nice fourteen-stoner on you! She'll walk you threadbare!'

"'Jerusalem! you're in for it!' sniggered a drain-pipe. 'Do you know who's wearing you? Why, Lot's wife! She's a Suffragette now, and when I tell you her feet move as fast as her tongue you know what's in store for you. Talk about rods in pickle!' and the drain-pipe went into a disgusting fit of laughter. 'Won't some one stop her?' I panted. 'Stop her!' screamed a dirty cat's tail I barely avoided treading on. 'Stop her! Why, nothing will stop her, she's got the latest improved turbine boiler! Take care she doesn't go too fast, that's all!' Scarcely were the words uttered before I found myself being whirled along at a terrific pace—up, down, dash, smash, through pebbles and puddles, on and on I flew, and I saw all around me thousands of other boots and shoes, all propelled by gigantic, never-tiring Suffragettes, who covered the ground with prodigious, elephantine bounds. This terrible punishment went on for days and nights, till I at length grew so thin that there was scarcely anything left of me. Sometimes I was baked, sometimes drowned, whilst, at all times, my inside and outside were torn and mangled. Then, to my immeasurable joy, I was kicked off, and for some brief moments enjoyed perfect rest. From this happy state I was abruptly awakened, to find myself sitting bound and gagged in a high-backed chair. Bending over me was a very tall and slender dentist with a big, round, babyish face and happy, innocent smile. In one hand he held a huge pair of forceps, and in the other the needle of the whirling instrument used for boring holes in teeth prior to filling them. 'I am Paul,' he said, 'and it is my unpleasant task to attend to your mouth every day. I shall first of all extract your teeth, then replace them, and, lastly, fill them. It will hurt you frightfully, but you must be patient; and I shall keep on at it till you cease swearing and begin of your own accord to repeat "The Old Hundredth," when your punishment will cease, and you will find yourself on the high road to Heaven. Now!' And ere I could stop him, he thrust the forceps into my mouth and began pulling. Pain! the pain was unendurable, inconceivable! All my previous sufferings were as nothing to it. And with the extraction of each tooth it increased. At last he stopped, and, with the perspiration trickling down his face, pointed to a bloody pile on the floor. 'There they are,' he said, 'thirty-two of them! The toughest to draw imaginable. Now I shall stick them in again and fill them!' He did so, and the torture was so great that over and over again I swooned. For twenty hours he whirled away first at one root and then at another, piercing the gums and pricking the nerves; and the more I implored him to stop the more he hurt me. At last he finished, the whirling instrument was laid aside, and with the tip of my bleeding tongue I felt, in each tooth, a hole big enough to hold an egg.

"'Do you see this?' he said, holding up a bottle. It's Scotch whiskey, and I'm going to fill your teeth with it. You will then know what it is to have your head full of alcohol and your stomach empty. You will smell it; its fumes will tickle your throat, and yet you will not be able to satisfy your cravings for it; and this punishment will continue till you earnestly repent of your misspent life.'

"He lifted up the bottle, and the next moment I felt its burning contents poured into the hollow of my teeth. It was in vain that I besought him for one drop, wherewith to moisten my parched throat. Not one drop did he spill, not one drop fell out; and not one drop could I remove wit the tip of my tongue, though my throat was ten thousand times more a-thirst than it had ever been before. The smell of the whiskey drove me mad. I prayed for it, I cried for it, I tore whole pieces out of my tongue as I beat and prodded it against the jagged edges of my teeth. But all to no purpose; my head remained full and my stomach empty.

"A whole lifetime seemed to pass in this tantalising, agonising manner, and then into the room, in Indian file, stalked all my friends and relations, each carrying in their hands a champagne glass. My uncle, who had been dead and buried at the very least thirty years, headed the procession. Walking solemnly up to me, he took hold of my nose, twisted it round like a tap, and down through my foaming mouth poured the whiskey. As soon as his glass was full he raised it above his head, and exclaimed in a sepulchral voice, 'Health! Health! Health!' to which all the company in chorus responded 'Amen! Amen! Amen!' One after another my relatives and friends followed his example, and twisted my nose till the whiskey flowed. And all the while the alcohol poured from me, and I saw them gulp it down, my thirst and craving for it grew, and I besought and implored them to spare me a drop—just one drop, one tiny drop. But they shook their heads, and murmured,

'Serve you right! Ask Paul, and see what he says.' And none of them pitied me, till my youngest niece, Dorothy, whom I had many a time in her childhood half scared to death by my tipsy antics, and who had lately joined the Salvation Army, came into the room, and, on seeing my mother-in-law slyly give my sore and bleeding nose a vicious twist, at once ran up to her and pulled her away, crying out, 'For shame! Poor uncle! See how you have hurt him!' And as she fetched some cold spring water, and bathed and bandaged me, I grew heartily ashamed of my past conduct towards her, and from the very depths of my heart asked her pardon. To my delight, she kissed me—the first true kiss of affection I had had for years; and no sooner did her lips touch my cheeks than quite voluntarily I began to chant 'The Old Hundredth.' As I did so, room and people vanished, and I found myself standing, strong and upright in the open air, bathed in the glorious light of a heavenly sunset; and in this delirium of joy I awoke. That was the dream, and its effect was such, that from that very night I never drank another drop of alcohol. I forthwith became enrolled in the Salvation Army, in which—praise be to God!—I have ever since remained."

CHAPTER VII

TALE DREAMS

I HAVE often dreamed complete tales, and, oddly enough, the scene of my tale-dream is, more often than not, in Hyde Park. I append the following by way of illustration.

I dreamed it was a wet night, and that I saw, sitting alone on a seat in Hyde Park, with the rain falling mercilessly on her head and shoulders, and forming a large puddle in her lap, a woman—a silent, white-faced woman, that might well have passed for a corpse, or for a typical phantasm of the dead. I was so struck with the sight that I involuntarily stopped, and, advancing towards her, enquired if she were ill.

The sound of my voice made her start, and, shaking the water from her dress with a dull, mechanical movement, she said reproachfully, "Why can't folks let me alone? You are the third who has spoken to me within the last half-hour. I came here to be alone—utterly alone—save for *him!*" and here she gave a kind of convulsive sob and stretched her hands appealingly before her. The woman interested me, and I felt that there was much in her that would furnish me with copy—copy for some article on real humanity, on the flotsam and jetsam of womanhood.

And so, instead of obeying her injunctions to go, I stayed.

"Tell me," I said persuasively, "your history. You can confide in me; I am old—old enough to be your"—then I thought of my bare thirty-seven summers, and blushed—"well, old enough to be your uncle. May I sit down?"

"The seats," she murmured, "are free to all. I can go!"

She rose, and I touched her gently on the arm. "Come!" I said, "you can trust me. I'm only a journalist in search of suitable material for my pen. It is wretchedly wet and cold out here; let us go to the nearest restaurant and have something nice and warm, and perhaps you will then tell me all about—*him*."

"Him!" she cried, with such a fierceness in her voice that I quailed. "*Him!* What do you know about *him?* He would have made two of such as you! But"—and the scorn in her tones died away—"I see you mean it kindly. Perhaps you *are* unlike the rest. Yes, I will trust you!

Take me to some shop where I can thaw, and I will tell you about—*him.*"

I dreamed we crossed the park and, taking a taxi to Victoria, found a restaurant where, for a moderate sum, I was able to procure her a solid meal—a meal that was a good deal too solid for me, but which she ate as only a girl in her station can eat; whilst I, looking on, watched the colour slowly creep back to her ashen cheeks, and the raindrops rise in minute vapour clouds from her skirt and boots.

"Now," she said, as she drained the last drop of coffee from her cup, and shook her head when I asked her if she would have any more, "now, you've kept your bargain and I'll keep mine. You asked me to tell you about him, and so I will. To begin with, by *him* I mean Jim Bailey—my young man Jim. But, of course, I suppose you've guessed that. Journalists know a thing or two—at least, so I've always understood. Well, in speaking of Jim I'm not going to beat about the bush; that wasn't his wish—not it! Jim was a burglar, mister, a real top-sawyer in his profession, and there wasn't his equal in London. I knew it when I first met him, and he knew all about me—that I was one of the cleverest filchers—pocket-pickers—in Whitechapel. Well, mister, we took to one another at first sight, and, after a few months courting, agreed that, if we were to marry and have a quiet time of it, we must give up our present line of business. Burglary is all very well for a single man, if he is 'pinched' no one misses him, but when it comes to seven years' penal for a man with a wife and half a dozen children, it isn't good enough. Jim and I were sensible enough to see that, mister, and we both came to the conclusion that, after one more haul, we would turn over a new leaf and live like respectable people. But what we wanted was five hundred pounds. If we had that sum we could retire to the country and run a farm. Jim liked an outdoor life, and I loved animals, so we thought a farm would suit us down to the ground.

"Well, it was my turn first. Biding my time I, at last, saw a safe opportunity. I mingled with a crowd of well-dressed ladies at a benevolent bazaar in the West End, and came home with five nice fat purses—close on a hundred and fifty pounds in hard cash. Not bad, was it ? I banked the money, and Jim, being a man of honour, told me that would do, and that I must now definitely retire on my laurels—a feat which he hoped soon to accomplish himself.

"One day Jim came to me in a great state of excitement. 'Lil,' he said, 'here's news ! The very thing we have been longing for has come to pass, and it is the softest job imaginable. What do you think? This afternoon, as I was taking forty winks in my wicker chair before the fire, there came a timid knock at the door, and in walked a lady!'

"'A lady, Jim!' I exclaimed. 'Not a real lady?'

"'She was, though,' Jim went on, 'a real lady bred and born. I could tell that the moment she opened her mouth—though I guessed as much from her dress, which was just moderate, nothing more. "I believe," she said, with a nervous little smile, "I'm speaking to Mr. James Bailey?" "That's right enough, ma'am," I replied, "I'm Jim Bailey and no one else."

"'"Well, Mr. Bailey," she said in slow, measured tones, as if she weighed each syllable in her mind very carefully before she spoke, "I have heard of you from the Rev. Mr. Towell." At the mention of the name of the chaplain at Dartmoor, Lil—you know the fellow who laid it on so thick when I was doing time there, three years ago last May—at the mention of his name, Lil, I jumped as if I had been shot.

"'"Then you're a lady missionary, are you?" I said, with a scowl. "If that's your game, all I can say is that you've come to the wrong shop. I don't cotton to prigs of that kidney."

" 'I spoke so savage, Lil, that the lady shook all over, and I saw her eyes flash round the room as if seeking the quickest avenue of escape. Then she suddenly grew calm, and, lifting her veil, stared me straight in the face. "Do I look like a missionary, Mr. Bailey ?" she said; "if so, you are the first person who has ever noted the likeness. Look!"

" 'Look! Why, I couldn't help looking, Lil; and with every respect to you, Lil, she was worth a good stare. She had golden hair, parted in the middle and brought low over her ears in the newest fangled fashion. Her eyebrows all but met over her nose, and she had a pair of the loveliest but hardest blue eyes I have ever seen. Lord save you!' Jim said, striking the palm of one of his hands with the fist of his other, 'they were hard—flint wasn't in it with them! And her mouth! That was cruel too—real downright cruel, with thin, tightly shut lips and sharp white teeth that glittered like a wolf's.

" 'But for all that she was beautiful—so beautiful that I thought I should never tire looking at her. Pooh! Lil, you needn't be jealous, old girl! She is none of my sort, anyhow.

" ' " Now ! " she exclaimed with a queer kind of snarl, as she took off the glove of her left hand so as to show me the tell-tale band of gold on the third finger—" now, Mr. Bailey, are you satisfied ? There is nothing of the missionary about me, is there ? " And when I saw the long, pointed nails, pink and polished like sea-shells, just as I've always been told they do them at the lady-barber's, I coughed. Observe my astuteness, Lil. I saw now that she was no prig from a church or chapel, but a member of what folks call " The Smart Set." Yet how did she know Mr. Towell, and what brought her here ? Was she one of us or a 'tec ?

" ' " I see I must explain myself," she said, pulling out a chair fron the table and sitting down. " Though I'm living in a big house in Park Lane, Mr. Bailey, I'm a poor woman. My husband has all the money, and not I."

" ' " That doesn't sound quite fair, ma'am," I muttered, not knowing exactly what other remark to make.

" ' " Fair ! of course it isn't fair ! " she snapped. " Nothing is fair, is it ? But come, I'm not here to expatiate on injustice. Have you ever been hard up, Mr. Bailey ? You have. Good ! Then you can sympathise with me. I am hard up—so hard up that I am anxious to sell my diamonds—a wedding present from my husband—and, being a wedding present and positively the only present he has ever given me, you can understand my difficulty. In short, I want to sell it, but dare not. Dare not, because my husband would never forgive me if I did. Now, Mr. Bailey, do you understand how I became acquainted with your old friend, Mr. Towell. I got to know him because I wanted to know you, and I remembered the robbery for which you were convicted—one of the cleverest and most daring cases of burglaries on record—and thinking that you were still at Dartmoor, I asked Mr. Towell to get me permission to see you. He informed me, however, that you were out of prison, but, at my request, obtained me your present address."

" ' "From the 'cops,' of course, ma'am ? " I interrupted, smothering a curse.

" ' She nodded.

" ' "Well, ma'am," I enquired a trifle surlily, "what is it exactly that you want me to do ? "

" ' Then she came a foot or two nearer and, fixing her brilliant eyes on me with a gaze I wouldn't care to face from any 'tec, she said, " I want you to commit a sham burglary at my house, and do your work in such a manner as will lead my husband to suppose that you have stolen the necklace.

In reality you mustn't touch anything, or else "—here a very ugly expression crept into the corners of her mouth—" or else," she went on, " but there, I must take you on your honour, Mr. Bailey. You will promise to bide entirely by my instructions, won't you ? "

" ' " Certainly, ma'am," I answered, " especially if you make it worth my while."

" ' " What would you consider worth your while ? " she asked.

" ' " Three hundred and fifty pounds, ma'am," I hazarded, praying to heaven she would give it me ; for that sum, don't you see, Lil, would just make up our five hundred. To my surprise, the lady smiled. " That seems rather exorbitant," she said ; " but there, I'm no good at business. You shall have it, cash down, as soon as you have played the requisite part. To-day is Tuesday, isn't it ? " Here she thought for a moment, puckering up her forehead into tiny white wrinkles and tapping the back of the chair with her pointed nails—bird's claws, I call them. " I have it ! " she suddenly burst out. " Sunday ! Yes, Mr. Bailey, you must come to my house on Sunday evening between seven and eight. See, here is the address and a plan of the house as well." She gave me an envelope—a common enough envelope for a lady in her position—and bid me master the contents. She then went into minute details of the "plant," and at last prepared to take her departure. My word, old girl, you should have seen the phiz she pulled when I asked if she would like a cup of coffee!

"'"I came here professionally, Mr. Bailey," she said, "and not socially. Please understand that." And she left me feeling more like a stalactite than a human being!'

"'Is that all, Jim?' I asked.

"'Yes, Lil, that's all for the present,' Jim replied. 'What do you think of it?'

"'Risky, Jim,' was my answer, 'risky. It may be a dodge on the part of the police.'

"Jim shook his head.

"'Don't think so, Lil,' he said. 'I thought of that, of course, the moment the lady spoke about Towell, but as soon as she mentioned her husband I knew she was genuine. The very thought of her old man was poison—the best actress in London couldn't have simulated such hatred. You can take it from me, Lil, the lady will keep her bargain if I keep mine.'

"'Still, it is risky, Jim,' I said; 'her husband might catch you.'

"'Not if I have even an average amount of

luck,' Jim persisted. 'Her arrangements are admirable. Say, Lil, you wouldn't keep me back, old girl? That extra three hundred and fifty pounds will just set us going.'

"It certainly was an allurement, and though I still felt very uneasy—why I don't know—I eventually yielded, and we spent the rest of the morning talking about our farm. Lord! how we did reckon on it!

"Well, Sunday came at last, and Jim stayed with me till it was time for him to make tracks for the lady's house. Then—well, mister, I will tell you the rest of the story in his own words: 'After saying good-bye to you, Lil,' Jim began, 'I shouldered my bag of tools, and, taking a taxi, drove to the Marble Arch. I got out there, and went by motor-'bus to Park Lane. I had no difficulty in finding the lady's house, and, entering the front door with the key she gave me, I crept upstairs to her bedroom.

"'No one was about, I couldn't even detect the sound of distant voices, and the house bore every appearance of being deserted.

"'The room I entered was large, and furnished most luxuriously. On the duchess-table, facing the brightly polished French bed, was a gorgeous array of silver-backed brushes, trinket boxes, hand-glasses, manicuring instruments, powder jars, and heaps of other costly articles, including several very valuable rings and bracelets, which were thrown about with the utmost carelessness ; and a strong smell of some subtle scent pervaded the whole apartment. Connected with the room, by means of a door to the right of the dressing-table, was a dressing-room, where the master of the house usually slept. I did not enter it, as the lady had given me strict injunctions not to do so.

" 'The safe, where the diamonds had always been kept, stood by the bedside on the top of a black oak chest, and as I set to work on it with my tools, I couldn't help laughing to think what a precious trick it was, searching for what I knew wasn't there—for what I knew only too well was safe and snug in the lady's keeping, if not actually on its way to Amsterdam to be sold !

" 'It did not take me many seconds to crack the lid of the safe open, and I had just done so, when there was a blaze of light, a loud shriek, and, on turning round, I saw the lady.

" ' "Softly, ma'am," I whispered, "you're a bit too soon ! You should have waited till I was ready to be off. I have kept my part of the bargain ; keep yours. Quick ! The three hundred and fifty pounds ! "

"'But, instead of giving it me, she burst out shrieking again, and, rushing to the door, shouted, "Help! Murder! Help!"

"'Then for the first time I suspected treachery, and determining she should lose something at all events, I swept everything worth having off the dressing-table into my tool-bag, and, making a dart for the window, was preparing to jump out of it, for it was wide open and the garden did not look more than twelve or so feet beneath it, when there was a sharp bang, and, the next instant, my right arm dropped helplessly to my side. There was another bang, and I lost the use of my left. Faint and dizzy from the loss of blood, and utterly bewildered at the unexpectedness of the onslaught, I staggered back, and, coming into collision with a chair, crashed heavily to the ground. The next instant there was a rush from the doorway, and a crowd of servants, men and women, were pommelling me without mercy.

"'It was in vain I reminded them I was wounded, it was in vain I implored them to desist. Whenever they left off, the voice of their dastardly mistress from the background goaded them on to fresh endeavours, and I verily believe they would have finished me off altogether had not half a dozen policemen burst into the room, and sent them to the right-about. I was then lifted up and my wounds attended to, whilst the lady poured forth her tale.

" ' " I was at dinner," she began, " when, hearing a noise upstairs——"

" ' " What sort of a noise ? " the sergeant asked.

" ' " Oh, a dull thud," the lady said, lying glibly. " Fearing that it might be my husband, who was lying down in the dressing-room as he was not very well, I rushed upstairs, and, on opening the door, saw this man in the act of breaking open the safe. I shrieked out, and he rushed towards the window. I fired, aiming purposely at his arms, so as to merely disable him. Alarmed by the noise, the servants came rushing up from the kitchen, and I ran to telephone to the police station. On my return, the man was still in the grasp of my servants."

" ' " And your husband, ma'am ? " the sergeant asked deferentially.

" ' " I haven't been in to see yet," the lady replied a trifle shamefacedly, as I thought. " Will you come with me, sergeant ? I—I—am so nervous lest anything should have happened to him."

" ' They entered the dressing-room together, and then—then as we all listened in breathless expectation, for I instinctively felt the sinister-eyed woman had planned some terrible drama, there was a heart-rending scream, and in spite of the remonstrances of the police, every one, saving myself and the constables who held me, made a rush for the door. The master of the house was lying on the floor beside his bed, face downwards, with the back of his skull smashed to pulp. " He did it with his jemmy, without a doubt," I heard some one say. " See, there are bloodstains on his coat ! "—which of course there were, stains from my own blood. Then the police sergeant formally charged me with the murder ; my clothes were searched, and all the trinkets I had nabbed from the dressing-table were brought to light.

" ' And all the while this was taking place, that demon of a traitress was kneeling beside her dead husband—the man she hated and whom, I am positive, she killed—moaning and groaning, and calling upon Heaven, in tones of the wildest grief, to let her die too !

" ' I stood no chance. It was useless to protest my innocence. No one believed me. I had been caught in the act of burglary ; who, then, could have murdered him but I ? The very idea of that delicate, heart-broken woman, that woman who was only too obviously almost out of her mind with grief, being the horrible monster I described her was ludicrous—so thin a story wouldn't deceive a baby.

"'The lady therefore scored all along the line; whilst I—I, her poor deluded tool—was marched straight away to jail.'"

Here the girl from the park paused.

"Well," I said gently, "and what is the sequel? Is Jim in prison still?"

"No," the girl answered dreamily; "Jim, my Jim, is free. He was hanged at six o'clock this morning!"—and as she said this I awoke.

The significant characteristics of this dream are as follows: Rain portends tears; coffee, severe criticism; robbery, illness; pale blue (in the eyes of the lady), impending trouble; diamonds, drowning. Money, minor ailments and surprise visits; murder, great danger; hanging, violent quarrels, separation and divorce.

The realisation of these prognostications worked out thus: Within a week of the dream I was deeply grieved at the death of an old friend; one of my books came in for very severe criticism; a near relation fell ill; the wife of one of my old schoolfellows was drowned under very painful circumstances; I received a visit from a man I had not seen for twenty years, who told me he had just been divorced; and as I drove back with him to the railway station our taxi collided with another, and we had a remarkably narrow escape of being killed.

I think it was about a year after I had this dream that I again dreamed a tale-dream, the introductory scene of which was also in Hyde Park.

I thought I was sauntering down one of the quietest and least-frequented of the side-walks that converge, and, meeting, form an angle at Hyde Park Corner, when I saw, sitting on a bench, a man whose mere outline instantly arrested my attention and enlisted my sympathy. As I approached, the gaslight caught his face and threw his features into such strong relief that I paused to look at him; and if ever I saw real, honest resentment at Fortune's capricious behaviour deep-rooted in a human countenance, I saw it in this man's. Here was no mere idler, no miserable whiner; here was a man who was up in arms against Providence, because he felt he had justifiable grounds of complaint.

He had a strong, massive frame, which, had it been decently nourished, would undoubtedly have marked him for a fine figure; he was too straight-limbed and square-shouldered for the working-man, too coarse-skinned and heavy-moulded for any possible specimen of the middle classes.

Taking the vacant seat at his side, I offered him some tobacco—for, though a rigid non-smoker myself, I invariably carry a few ounces of the highly treasured weed with me on my nocturnal wanderings, as also a neat little pocket revolver in case of blackmailers and other undesirables—and soon had the gratification of hearing him unburden himself. "I can work if I want to," he admitted with the utmost candour; "every strong man can. To say the unskilled labourer can't get a job is all bosh! There are a dozen and one jobs of a sort always open to him, only he prefers to live on his wife and children, and—loaf. No, I'm not that sort. That's not on my programme. I'm not working because, for the present, I haven't the heart to work. I've been jilted by luck, and I feel too sore to ask for employment. Yes," he said, with a sudden spurt of enthusiasm, "I'll tell you all about it.

"Some months ago I belonged to the police force at Dulwich. I was on night duty, and had been particularly enjoined to keep an eye on a certain house, the owner of which, a rich banker, was away in the South of France. Night after night I passed by the house, and, as far as I could tell, everything was in order. You know the police have orthodox dodges for seeing if premises have been entered, and I, of course, made use of them. Well, one evening—it was in October, and the shadows from the big trees, lining the road outside the house, lay so thick around me, that I could stand among them without being seen by any one from a distance—I came on the round at nine o'clock, and on arriving at the house I kept an eye on, was not a little surprised to find the shutters of the front sitting-room open, the blinds up, and the table laid for dinner. This rather astonished me, as we had received no intimation at the police station that the family were back. The room looked so warm and cosy, and the good things on the table so extremely appetising, that I could not refrain from stopping for what I intended should be a few seconds and looking at them.

"Now I don't suppose, sir, for one minute that many members of the force take much interest in table-laying, but with me it was different. My wife had formerly been a cook in good families in the West End, and I had often gone out waiting; so that I had a pretty correct notion of what's what, and could sum up the social status of a family in the twinkling of an eye, if I could get but one peep at the setting of their dinner-table.

"What I saw in this instance perplexed me: The owner of the house was supposed to be a gentleman in a good position, but the setting of the cloth was the worst I've ever seen. To begin with, the serviettes were put on anyhow; indeed, I noticed that there were one or two short—the table was set for six, and I could only count four serviettes. Then there was an unnecessary amount of silver, both table and sideboard literally groaning under the weight of it. A huge, old-fashioned silver stand, containing one big fruit dish and four small ones, stood in the centre of the table, whilst all round were big silver cake dishes. To each place there were at least five too many forks and spoons, whilst on the sideboard was the most vulgar (you see, sir, I understand the real use of that word) display of silver bowls, cups, entrée and bon-bon dishes, knives, forks, and spoons I ever have seen. The sole idea of the hostess seemed to be to impress her visitors with a sense of her wealth—she had, so to speak, purposely made an exhibition of it.

"I was so interested in my observations that, quite unconsciously, I left the shelter of the trees, and, stepping up to the railings, leaned over them. I was now close to the window, the lower panes of which were almost on a level with my face, and, as I peered through it, a tall man in evening dress entered the room. 'Mr. Montague, I suppose,' I murmured to myself, mentioning the name of the banker. 'Why, he's actually wearing red socks, and has a coloured handkerchief and a sixpenny ready-made tie!' You see, sir, I notice every detail in a gentleman's dress; and, as you doubtless know, nothing gives a show away so much as loud-coloured handkerchiefs and ready-made ties; no one in tip-top society wears such things.

"Now I didn't know much about bankers, as most of the people at whose houses I visited were real gentry, but I never should have believed that even a moderately well-to-do business man would have dressed like that. I was gazing at him in astonishment, when he suddenly approached the window, and, seeing me, threw up the sash. 'Are you the policeman,' he said, 'who has been keeping an eye on this house during my absence?'

"'Yes, sir,' I replied, not a little embarrassed, for I felt I had done rather a mean thing in thus spying on him.

"'I am really very much obliged to you,' he went on, 'for I find everything is all right; but come in for a moment, I can't talk to you out there.' Now, as you are aware, sir, the pay of a policeman is no great shakes—not as much by a long way as that of an ordinary mechanic, who has no responsibilities and very little education—so that when the gentleman fingered his waistcoat-pocket I had visions of something that might come in very useful for my wife and kiddy. Without unduly singing my own praises, I'm not as selfish as many working men. I only had one child, because I knew full well I couldn't afford to keep more. Of course it was wrong of me to think of taking a tip for merely having done my duty, and it was wrong of me also to leave my beat, even for a moment; but then we are all prone to weakness at times, sir,—even Prime Ministers and Home Secretaries. Moreover, I must admit that, apart from the thought of a possible sovereign, I was curious to see inside a so strangely ordered household, and the smell of the dinner to a half-empty stomach was very tantalising—prime roast mutton, onion sauce, pheasant, fish and tripe—an odd assortment, sir, but only in keeping with the arrangement of the cloth. The gentleman met me at the door, and insisted on my stepping inside. 'You can scent the good things, can't you, Bobby?' he laughed, 'and you may bet your whiskers they are good, too!' he added, smacking his lips. 'Better than they give you at home, eh?'

"'Yes, sir,' I replied. 'We can't afford much in the way of meat, one joint has to last us a week; and as for the entrées—well, we generally manage to do without them.'

" 'Just so!' the gentleman smiled, 'and that is why I am going to give you a treat to-night. In spite of the fact that I'm a pretty well-to-do banker—regular City man, don't you know—I'm in my heart of hearts a bit of a Socialist: don't believe in class distinction and all that sort of thing, like to see the poor man enjoying himself as well as the rich. Why the deuce shouldn't he? the same God made them both. I am just letting you know my sentiments so that you need not be surprised at my asking you into my dining-room, which I have observed you admiring from the road for some little time. Oh! bother the sergeant, he won't see you, and you need only stay a few minutes, just to taste a bit of the good fare which you will find every bit as good as it smells.' He badgered me so, sir, that in the end I gave in, and after assuring myself that the sergeant was nowhere about, I slipped through the doorway and into the dining-room. The gentleman very thoughtfully drew down the blind, and, bidding me be seated, left the room.

" 'Well,' I said to myself, 'here's a pretty go and no mistake! Here I am, P.C. Hardy K. 202, supposed to be on his beat, stumping along towards the Common—instead of which he is the guest of Leslie Montague, Esq., one of the best-known bankers in London. I examined the cutlery—the best firm in Sheffield, of course; the glass—nothing under-half-a-crown apiece; the serviettes—Damask linen every one of them; and I was about to slip out of my seat and examine the pile of things on the sideboard, when the door opened and a footman, carrying a tray laden with dishes, entered. Following at his heels were Mr. Montague and a lady, who, from the very affectionate manner in which Mr. Montague addressed her, I gathered was his wife.

"And here let me say that I only concluded she was a lady from the fact of her being Mrs. Montague, otherwise her attire, which was flash and fast in the extreme, would have led me to believe she was some very common person. I'm no judge of ladies' dress, and couldn't perhaps tell a real, soft satin from the inferior quality, I've heard my wife call papery stuff; but I do know a flaming scarlet velvet bodice with a shortish yellow skirt and high-heeled patent leathers are as out of place in most gentlemen's houses as a pair of bishop's pants would be in mine.

"But then, of course, they were Socialists, and there is no accounting for anything, so I have always been told, among that class of people.

"'Good evening, constable,' she said to me,

smiling all over her rubicund face and making the trinkets on her bracelets rattle like half-a-dozen bead curtains. 'My husband and I are so very much obliged to you for taking such care of our house during our absence, and we think the least we can do in return is to invite you to join us at dinner, after which my husband intends making you a little present. Are you fond of roast mutton?'

"'Yes, ma'am,' I replied, feeling very hungry all of a sudden, for the smell of all those good things I have told you about, sir, really made my mouth water.

"'And tripe?' she went on.

"Again I answered, 'Yes.'

"'Then that is all right,' she said, with a sigh of relief. 'My husband and I ordered what we fancied you would most appreciate—a good, homely fare and plenty of it—so don't be afraid to have a second helping. Now, Willie dear, let us begin.'

"Well, sir, we all sat down. It was by far the queerest meal I have ever had, and I cannot say I enjoyed it, for the meat was tough and the vegetables half raw. But there was no help for it. When I had got one plateful down and was congratulating myself that I could now give my jaws a spell of rest, they piled me up another; and it was not until I had at last eaten enough meat, even to satisfy them, they allowed me respite.

" 'Well, Policeman,' they said, 'we are indeed overjoyed at your appetite; it is, after all, only in accordance with your size—you are a big man—very. And now for the pudding.'

" At the mention of pudding, sir, I could barely restrain a groan. Pudding! why, there wasn't the fraction of an inch in my middle, that wasn't stretched to bursting point with grisly bits of mutton and hard wedges of potato. But what could I do? They begged and implored me not to be shy! I had a large frame, and should of necessity have a large appetite. It was in vain I told them I had had enough, they simply wouldn't hear of it. The pudding came, an enormous suet roly-poly—spotted monkey, my kiddie calls it—bathed in butter sauce. Now, to tell you the truth, sir, it's rather a favourite pudding of mine, still they need not have given me half of it. And then, sir, when I had helped the last piece down with my fork and was feeling like a stuffed Christmas stocking, on came dessert and wine.

" 'What! you won't have a glass of port?' Mrs. Montague cried, looking at me with a pained expression in her big, innocent blue eyes. 'Oh, you must have one, Constable, just one! Come, you can't refuse a lady!'

"'The sergeant, ma'am!' I gasped, for I could hardly articulate a sound owing to the pudding and—potatoes; 'if the sergeant smells port, ma'am, I shall be discharged!'

"'You needn't be afraid of that, Constable,' Mrs. Montague laughed. 'We will give you some peppermints, which I can guarantee will kill the smell of any port! Come, now, don't be churlish!'

"I gave in, sir. It was wrong of me, I know, but what else could I do? They filled my glass; not once, but three or four times, and I drank it up, every drop—greedily! for the mutton, which was uncommonly salt, had made me very thirsty.

"'Then, sir, I looked at my watch and saw to my horror that I had only three minutes left; that is to say, I was expected to meet the sergeant in three minutes time. A quarter of a mile in three minutes, could I do it? If not, then——" and here the man on the bench snapped his fingers emphatically—"I should be fined and dismissed the force! A quarter of a mile in three minutes! Fastish walking in a heavy overcoat and thick regulation boots, isn't it?

"Well, sir, I got up and tried to stand, but my— I couldn't. The port had got into my head, my back, my knees—all over me—and I'm blessed if I didn't tumble into my chair with a thud. Ten times I made the attempt and ten times I failed, growing feebler and feebler, and drowsier and drowsier after each effort.

"If ever anyone underwent the sufferings of the damned I did then, for muddled and fuddled as I was, I retained for some moments sufficient intelligence to depict what would happen, if I failed to meet the sergeant. At length, however, sleep overcame me, and realising with a groan what was happening, I sank deep down in the soft folds of the luxurious easy chair, and lost consciousness.

"When I came to myself it was dawn. A few straggling beams of cold grey light, pouring in through the light blinds, enabled me to recognise my surroundings. I was still in the armchair, and before me on the table lay the dessert and wine.

"Every vestige of silver had gone; and so had my host and hostess." Here the man on the bench laughed bitterly. "I was duped, of course!" he added; "the man and the woman were no more Mr. and Mrs. Montague than they were Red Indians! They were part of a gang of notorious burglars who had been wanted for a long time!"

"Good Heavens!" I cried, "they were caught?'

"Caught, yes," the man on the bench hissed; "seven years apiece, and as for me—I got dismissed! Dismissed! and I have not had the heart to look for another job since!"

I gave him five shillings—all I had with me—which he accepted gratefully, and I left him there muttering—muttering that it was I who had been duped—not he—he had never been in the police force at all—which so annoyed me, that I awoke!

In this dream the significant features (which were fully verified afterwards) are as follows: Tobacco portends a visit to the seaside; a policeman, loss of a pet animal or some much-treasured article; silver, a present of flowers or vegetables; knives a quarrel; red (in the socks and handkerchief), great changes; yellow (in the lady's dress), treachery on the part of a friend; jewellery in general, trouble; eating, an accident to the teeth; drinking, a visit to a place of entertainment; the swoon, danger from lightning; burglars, breakages; money, minor ailments and a surprise visit.

When staying in York Road, Westminster, some years ago, I had the following dream—and I think a more vivid one I have never dreamed. I fancied I was borne at a terrific speed through every description of varied scenery, in a country that was entirely new to me. I saw bare mountains rising to a prodigious height; wide plains where never a blade of grass grew; great sweeps of prairie alive with every kind of vegetable life; slow rivers, narrow rapid streams, and cataracts of hellish fury; forests of pines, moaning as in a hurricane; trees with strange faces like living things; woods full of flowers and peopled by maidens of exquisite beauty; meadows bathed in sunlight; and lofty cities built of coloured marble.

And I was borne past all these and set down at the entrance to a sombre city, whose black and silent streets re-echoed to my footsteps. Cold with fear, —for every building I saw was black, and destitute of any sign of life, whilst overhead the blue sky had turned to an intense grey—I hurried on, urged whither I knew not. It seemed to me that I was seeking some familiar spot—some known harbour of refuge against a vague, unimagined danger that pursued me; and, as I pressed forward, the air grew more and more oppressive. Then I met things—horrible things with clammy hands that tried to keep me back; and as I felt their loathsome touch and fœtid breath a great weakness filled my limbs.

"God of mercy!" I cried, "help me, and keep me from these."

Then in some inexplicable manner a new strength came into my body. Taking courage, I leaped forward; I hurled aside my assailants, and I could hear them mocking and cursing as I broke through them.

Just as the haven I longed for came in sight—and I know not what it was or how I knew it—I saw a beautiful maiden with golden hair and great, deep blue eyes, who was evidently waiting for me and who beckoned me with arms that, white as ivory, gleamed against the blackness of everything around her. Only a few feet separated us. I gathered up my limbs to take a final spring and—with a sigh of satisfaction, I felt her soft arms encircle me. It was a moment of infinite paradise. Then a hot, pitiless hand was laid upon my neck and I was hurled backward from her clasp—my head struck the ground, and blankness swallowed me again. When consciousness returned, all was changed. A wonderful sensation of liberty, as it were of transition from the material to the ethereal, possessed me. At my feet lay the thing of flesh and blood which had served me as a body, and, to my horror, I saw bending over it a creature of copper hue—a man in build and form, but enormous in size and development. "See thy future!" it cried; and my free soul felt a strange pang of pity at the sight of its face—it was so full of sorrow that I could not fathom; a vastness of pain that could only be immortal. Yet as I looked, my pity was changed to fear and hate; the creature became contorted with demoniac fury; its lips wreathed and twisted, its eyes flashed, and it cried aloud so that my soul longed to flee yet dare not.

"See! see!" it shrieked. And I looked and saw myself. It was I, but how altered! I was an aged man sitting alone in a dreary attic, bathed in a flood of cold moonlight, waiting—waiting for what? I looked a little further and saw a muddy river, and over it hovered the form of death.

"Art thou satisfied?" asked my tormentor, "satisfied, or wouldst thou see more of the days to come? Destiny, Destiny, Destiny! It rules the world, from the infant's cradle to the roar of the guns or—a watery grave. And thou hast seen Destiny. Wake and regard it as fancy if thou wilt. Stifle it, bury it, drown it. Thou hast seen what thou hast seen, and—it is Destiny!"

The creature's voice rose higher and higher, then dropped, and dropped, till it died out altogether. And as it died out, the horrid phantom vanished, and, in its place, rose a mass of red and curling flames, that in letters of fire wrote, in mid-air: "Art thou going to the ZONE ARTO?"

A reply rose irresistibly to my lips.

"Ere eight hours chime," I said, like one repeating

a parrot lesson. And, as I spoke, I felt my despised body draw me back, and I entered into it, and experienced again the sensation of the sleeper returning to the living world.

Then I dreamed I awoke, and lay in bed striving, in vain, to recall my own answer to that question of fire. It had slipped so readily from my lips, and it had slipped with equal readiness from my brain. I could only repeat, again and again, the meaningless question, " Art thou going to the ZONE ARTO ? "

The sun was high and hot. I dreamed I rose leisurely, and, led by an invisible agency, made my way to the coffee-room of an adjacent restaurant. Sitting there was a man who, from his appearance, might have been an Italian of doubtful class, possibly one of the anarchists of whom Europe at that moment stood in dread. His companion was a girl, with dark hair and blue eyes, tall and beautifully dressed.

As I sat down the latter looked up, and I saw, or fancied I saw, a sudden liking for me sparkle in her blue eyes, so that my heart went out to her straight. I was not accustomed to be noticed by women, and her interest was pleasant in my loneliness. Probably my face showed her what I thought, for she lowered her eyes quickly, with just the ghost of a smile on her full red lips.

This exchange of glances did not escape the man's observation. He frowned at me in such a menacing manner that I felt apprehensive as to his next movements; he was evidently jealous, whence I inferred that he must be either the husband or lover of the pretty girl; and ridiculous as it may seem, I rebelled against the idea, and began to form plans for freeing her from him, for—I assured myself—he was unworthy of her love.

I would insult him, pick a quarrel, fight a duel—and pose in her eyes as the conquering hero! This and much more nonsense rushed through my brain, as I ate my frugal meal and watched the two.

Suddenly I was forced by some unrestrainable impulse, and, as much to my own surprise as theirs, I leaned forward and whispered, "Are you going to the ZONE ARTO?"

The effect was marvellous

The man dropped his cup with an oath—the hot coffee soaking through his trousers made him wince with pain—and the girl gazed at me with dilated eyes.

"Good God!" she ejaculated, a slightly foreign accent in her voice only adding to her charm, "are you one of us?"

It was my turn to be amazed and puzzled.

Was I one of them? What did she mean? Was

it possible that my dream was no idle thing and that the haunting words had some deep signification? Out of pure mischief and curiosity I nodded a grave assent. "Do you intend to go?" I added.

"Ere eight hours chime," was her reply; and the words brought with them a perfect recollection of my own dream-answer. Then I saw again the brown form and the brown river; and shuddered. The girl, I was sure from her face, perceived the tremor that made the cup and saucer I held vibrate in my nervous grasp.

Meanwhile; the eyes of the man had never ceased to scrutinise me; I felt them like burning points. What an ill-looking ruffian he was—sinister and repulsive, jealous as Othello; and ready, I felt sure; for any pretext whatsoever to assassinate me.

I was not surprised when he addressed me, and his voice was in admirable keeping with his person.

"If you belong to the society; signor; where is your insignia?"

He put his elbows on the table, leaned his face on his hands; and fixed me with his great angry eyes. The question naturally staggered me. I had no answer, no excuse, no clue to its meaning; but the same strange inspiration seized me, and letting myself go, as it were; I calmly answered,

"I was sent to meet you here."

He was still suspicious. "By whom?" he snapped.

This was a poser. But it flashed across my mind that a few minutes before I had heard the girl mention the name "Dusetto." She had articulated it so prettily that it caught my attention; and I ventured to pronounce it now, noticing its effect on both with a quiet smile. Still the man was not satisfied, and I was wondering how long I could bluff the matter out, when the girl came to my rescue. Laying her little hand on his sleeve she gave him a look—just one glance from her eyes, as a woman very sure of her ground can do—and said to me emphatically,

"Then command us. What can we do for you?"

"Well," I said, trusting to luck and coolness to see me through. "I wish to accompany you to the Zone Arto. I have not yet been, and wish to repair the omission at the first opportunity."

The girl gave her companion another quieting glance. Then, addressing me with a curious mixture of friendliness and distrust, she said, "We shall be pleased to have you with us; we are going to-night."

I was overjoyed. The adventure now seemed full of possibilities, and I was asking eagerly where I should meet them, when the Italian interfered.

"If you would mind your own business we should be the better pleased to mind ours," he hissed; adding maliciously before the girl could stop him, "the signor doubtless knows his own English proverb, 'Two's company, three's none.'"

Perhaps it was the man's manner more than his words that stung me, but, however that may be, my wrath was roused, and I should have made a passionate reply had not the door of the coffee-room swung open, and a whole bevy of customers entered.

There was no possibility of continuing the conversation, and the man and girl, quickly finishing their meal, rose to go.

"Meet me outside the Waterloo Hotel at 6.30," the girl whispered, with a little trill of laughter. "You know, in Poverty Corner."

"Of course," I replied in a low voice; "I would go anywhere to meet you."

Accordingly at 6.30, I dreamed, I went to the place of assignation. After waiting there for some time, I had just decided to go away when the girl, looking more beautiful than ever, suddenly appeared. "Come along," she cried, touching me lightly on the arm, "come along, and I will take you to the Zone Arto." She signalled to a hansom, and, before I realised what was happening, I found myself being whirled along through street after street, through narrow byways, and crowded thoroughfares. On and on we went, till we finally arrived at a river wharf, where, rising and falling on the ebbing tide, was a boat containing a couple of dark-visaged, fiery-eyed men in vermilion caps, to whom my companion beckoned. They drew up to a flight of stone steps and we took our seats behind them. In absolute silence, we glided over the murky bosom of the Thames, which was singularly devoid of shipping, and at length drew up alongside a low, rakish-looking steamer, whose sides and funnel were painted black. A gigantically tall man with huge, cat-like eyes met us as we stepped on deck, and, at a sign from the girl, escorted us down the companion-way. For some seconds he paused outside the door of what I took to be the state cabin; and appeared to be straining his ears to catch sounds proceeding from within. Then, apparently satisfied that all was right, he threw open the door, and, the next instant, I found myself in a dimly lighted apartment full of tall, silent; hooded figures.

Anything more sinister and terrifying than this spectacle I could never have conceived. A cold sweat burst out all over my body. I turned to escape, but the door was shut and guarded. I was entirely at the mercy of the assembly.

"He has come to see the Zone Arto," laughed the girl.

"And he shall see it!" murmured a dozen hollow and assumed voices. "But first blindfold him." Instantly, one of the figures stepped noiselessly up to me, and producing a green sash, bound it securely over my eyes. I was then swung round three times, and, the sash being suddenly removed, I found myself standing in a meadow—hooded figures, girl, cabin, ship had vanished—surrounded by nothing but grass—grass of the richest emerald green. The sun was shining, the sky was blue and cloudless, and the air, which was heavily laden with the sweet scent of clover and newly-mown hay, reminded me in no small degree of the country through which I had so lately travelled in my dreams.

"Well!" I said to myself as soon as I fully realised where I was, "it is quite certain I am not intended to fathom the secret of the Zone Arto. They could not have sent me to a safer place. I wonder where on earth I am!"

And then there arose a curious sound—a prolonged sound in which all nature seemed to join, and whisper, "The Zone Arto! The Zone Arto! This is the Zone Arto! You have returned whence you came. You have returned to the Zone Arto."

And as I listened in sore perplexity, the space all around me filled with the forms of countless men and women—composed of vibrating molecules of light. And the whisper continuing, I distinctly heard, "These are radio-activities, the essences of life. The society of the Zone Arto alone knows the secret of their creation, and alone knows how to extract them from the material body. Souls, ghosts, phantasms—terms by which you are accustomed to designate the superphysical—all are radio-activities. You are one of them yourself now."

"What!" I cried. "Do you mean I am no longer material?"

"Yes!" the whisper replied, "pro tempus, you are no longer physical. The Zone Arto Society extracted your radio-activity from your material body, and the latter is now lying at the bottom of the Thames."

"In other words, they murdered me!" I said.

"Yes," the whisper echoed, "if you prefer to use so harsh an expression, they murdered you! And they are now deliberating what physical body you shall next inhabit! Good-bye!"

And with "Good-bye" ringing in my ears I awoke.

In this dream (the following features have

already been fulfilled) :—Being borne through the air signifies falling in love; the bare mountains, change of occupation; the plains, state of tranquility; slow-flowing rivers, happiness; rapid rivers, difficulties; cataracts, great troubles; pine trees, death, illness, or a journey abroad; flowers in general, the forming of friendship; beautiful maidens, thoughts of suicide; sunlight, success in love, legacies and presents; marble, death; black in streets, &c., illness and death; grey in sky, trouble and danger from unexpected quarters; golden hair of girl, success; deep blue in girl's eyes, reconciliation, recovery from illness; the hand, a great change; copper hue of man, advent of someone connected with art; moonlight, illness, domestic and financial troubles, also death by drowning; muddy river, trouble; red flames, quarrels, voyages, great changes and accidents; fire, danger from water; the swarthy Italian, loneliness; the beautiful girl, thoughts of suicide; eating, accident to the teeth; brown in river, trouble; the meadow, tranquility; sunshine, success in love; blue sky, reconciliation, recovery from illness; green of grass, success in the arts.

But to certain other features, namely—the horrible Things with the clammy hands, the reference to Destiny, the Zone Arto, eight o'clock and half-past six, the steamer, the tall man with the cat-like eyes, the hooded figures, and the whisper —which owing to their vividness should be every whit as significant as those that have been already interpreted and fulfilled, I have, up to the present; been unable to attach any meaning.

INDEX

Accidents, 46
Afflicted, The, 81–92
Animals, 9–45, 120–124
Ants, 32

Balloons, 47
Bats, 9–12
Bears, 12–14
Bees, 32
Beetles, 33
Birds, 14–19
Births, 46
Bridges, 47
Bulls, 19
Butterflies, 33

Castle, 102–106
Cats, 20–22
Caterpillars, 33
Centipedes, 34
Colours, 47–49
Contemporary Events, 129–135
Corpses, 50
Cows, 22
Crocodiles, 22

Dancing, 49
Dead, 135–139
Deaf and Dumb, 83
Deaths, 50
Deer, 22
Digging, 51
Dogs, 22–25
Donkeys, 26
Dragonflies, 34
Dress, 51
Drinking, 52
Drowning, 52–53

Earwigs, 34
Eating, 54
Elephants, 45

Falling, 54
Finding things, 54
Fires, 58
Fish, 26–29
Flies, 45
Flowers, 55–56
Flying, 59
Forest, 94
Foxes, 29–30
Frogs, 30
Fruit, 58
Funerals, 50

Gnats, 34

Hanging, 70
Horses, 30–32
Hotch-Potch Dream, 74–78
Huntsmen, 112–120
Hyde Park Dreams, 151–179

Idiots, 84

Illness, 91–92
Insane, 84
Islet, 97

Kangaroos, 36

Ladybirds, 34
Leopards, 37
Lions, 36

Madness, 60
Maggots, 35
Marriage, 61
Mice, 37
Money, 62
Monkeys, 37
Moon, 61
Moths, 35
Murder, 62–63
Murderers, 85–91

Naked Dreams, 64–69
News from the Invisible World, References to, 86, 128

Panthers, 37
Phantastic Dreams, 93–124
Pigs, 38
Presents, 71
Professions, 70
Pumas, 37

Rags, 71
Rams, 42
Rats, 39
Religious Dreams, 140–150
Repetitionary and Peculiarly Vivid Dreams, 125–150

Sheep, 41
Sleep, 71
Slugs, 35
Snails, 35
Snakes, 40
Spiders, 35
Stags, 42
Storm, 110–112
Suicide, 73
Sun, 71

Tale Dreams, 151–192
Theatres, 118
Tigers, 43
Toads, 45
Towns, 100
Travelling, 72, 106–109
Trees, 57–58

Vegetables, 58

Wasps, 36
Water, 74
Weather, 74
Wolves, 44
Worms, 36

Zone Arts, Dream of the, 179–192